There

There

Lois Green, R.N., M.S.S.W., C.M.S.W. with N. Newell Rhodes

iUniverse, Inc.
New York Lincoln Shanghai

There

Copyright © 2005 by N. Newell Rhodes

All rights reserved. No part of this book may be used or reproduced by any means, graphic, electronic, or mechanical, including photocopying, recording, taping or by any information storage retrieval system without the written permission of the publisher except in the case of brief quotations embodied in critical articles and reviews.

iUniverse books may be ordered through booksellers or by contacting:

iUniverse
2021 Pine Lake Road, Suite 100
Lincoln, NE 68512
www.iuniverse.com
1-800-Authors (1-800-288-4677)

"Love is" Music by J. Martin Johnson
Lyrics by Susan Farris and Jean Mann Johnson
© 2001/2002
Candilane Publishing—BMI
Count Far Publishing—Seasac

ISBN: 0-595-33440-7 (pbk)
ISBN: 0-595-66933-6 (cloth)

Printed in the United States of America

This book is dedicated to all who helped shape my life, both professionally and personally. No matter how much or how little time I spent with you, our lives became interwoven, and you gave me an enormous gift. You opened your homes, your hearts, and your souls to me, and from your strength and willingness to go to that place of death and dying, you led me to *There.* Thank you.

Lois Green Palmer

Contents

PROLOGUE 1
CHAPTER 1 5
CHAPTER 2 12
CHAPTER 3 15
CHAPTER 4 26
CHAPTER 5 34
CHAPTER 6 37
CHAPTER 7 42
CHAPTER 8 51
CHAPTER 9 57
CHAPTER 10 59
CHAPTER 11 64
CHAPTER 12 69
CHAPTER 13 73
CHAPTER 14 100
AFTERWORD 105

ACKNOWLEDGMENT

What an honor it has been to have Lois Green Palmer as a friend. I thank this kind spirit for the privilege of writing her story.

I thank her husband, Wayne Palmer, for his help and support in this project.

I thank Bob Rhodes for bringing Lois into our lives and for giving me the tools to make this happen.

I thank Marian Washburn, Pat Pingry, Marian Perutelli, Stanley E. Hime, Sally Lee, Alberta Tolbert, Jim Kent, Rita Garner, and Nan Kluesner for their help in editing this work.

I thank Martha Morgan, Margaret Johnson, Sherry Lawler, Patti Zimmerman, Kathy Felts, Patricia McPherson, and Marie Maxwell.

I thank Paul Green III, Steve Davidson, Dr. Eric Raesky, Dr. Malcolm Lewis, Dr. Pat Maxwell, and Jeff Sinks.

I thank Ethel Peak, Francis and Wallace Boswell, Tip and Biddy Crutcher, Gwen Healey, and Phyllis Clary.

I thank J. Martin Johnson, Jean Mann Johnson, and Susan Farris.

I thank Felice Apolinsky, Anne Barker, Jennifer DeVille, Annemarie and Howard Harrod, Amon McDonald, Karen Wheeler, and all the wonderful souls from Gilda's Club who enriched my life by their love and support. What a blessing I have received from this experience.

Nancy Newell Rhodes

PROLOGUE

"The question most asked is 'How do you get there?' *There* being comfortable with death and enthusiastic about living when you have an illness for which there is no cure." This was September 20, 2000, and Lois Green, R.N., M.S.S.W., C.M.S.W., was at Gilda's Club Nashville facilitating a new program called "Living with Dying."

"Not a single part of me wants to leave this earth," Lois continued, sitting yoga-fashion on a love seat facing the group, "but three years ago my cancer returned. I refused chemotherapy because my energy level was so high and I felt so good. For two years I did have anti-hormone therapy, but I am interested in the quality of life, not a prolonged life with debilitating side effects from some treatment.

"During this time I began talking to folks about 'Living with Dying.' I have given many lectures on this subject, and NewsChannel 5 had me on their program that deals with health issues. They are doing a documentary and will be with me until the end." She took a sip of water. "I am hoping this information can be used as a learning tool."

She held up an autograph book. "I also brought my Love Book. I started this some time ago and have dozens now. There are wonderful messages, some pictures, and even dirty jokes." She smiled. "Write in it if you want, but don't feel obligated," she said and laid it on the coffee table in front of her. "I read through them whenever I need a boost.

"A year ago the cancer became more aggressive," Lois continued, "and I was told I had a month to live if I didn't take chemo. I still refused, but when I began to have pain and nausea, I called my doctor." She laughed, "What did I have to lose?

"Right now I am taking Zaloder with good results. I am symptom free, the chemo is working, and some of the tumors are smaller. I have no side effects, try to run two miles every day, and go bike riding whenever I can.

"But when this chemo stops working, I will not choose to try another; so I realize that at any time I could be within one to three months of dying."

Lois began her story. "I am a cancer survivor, having first had breast cancer in 1987. It returned nine years later. I did not worry when this happened because I had done so well previously. I had reconstructive surgery, as I had had with my first mastectomy; and when I went for my final visit, expecting to be dismissed, I asked the plastic surgeon to check out what I thought was the edge of an implant.

"He said, 'No, that's not what it is.' After a CAT scan, the cancer was found to have metastasized in my liver.

"I faced the fact I would soon be dying. I did not intend to die saying I wish I had done this or that. So my husband and I went rafting down the Grand Canyon, experienced Canada, saw Alaska, and celebrated my birthday with a five hour motorcycle ride on the Blue Ridge Parkway. And in Key West, I swam with the dolphins."

Lois then asked the members of the new group to tell their stories, and as they did, she encouraged them to say just how they felt about living with cancer. There were five survivors and two caregivers. Each spoke amid tears and laughter.

"Death is a human event which each person will eventually experience," Lois said, "and because of our diagnosis, it may be sooner for some of us than others." Lois thanked everyone for coming, then said, "But for whatever time I have left, I plan to keep on enjoying this beautiful world." She stood up. "I will see you next week."

She looked at the young man of twenty-nine who was battling a malignant brain tumor. "Give me a hug before I have to slap you," she said, and her beautiful smile lit up the room as she walked over and put her arms around him.

The members, meeting Lois for the first time, saw a lively, very pretty woman, so enthusiastic and full of life she did not appear to be the least bit ill. This is the story of Lois Green and how she got to *There.*

1

"Ann-ie Lois," the young mother called, dragging out the name in the lazy manner attributed to most southerners. Frankie walked to the edge of the porch and called again, "Ann-ie Lois!"

The dark-haired little girl winced. She put her hands on her hips and stamped her foot. "I hate it," she muttered before shouting back, "Call me Lois, and I'll come."

The mother laughed and called softly, "Lois, supper is ready."

Lois smiled, showing perfect white teeth, and her hazel eyes twinkled as she ran home.

Lois: **I always hated my name. I felt like everyone was calling me Auntie Lois. I had it legally changed to Lois Ann when my son was born.**

Lois and her mother were boarding with the Butler family on a small farm in Shelbyville, Tennessee. Frankie had moved back home after her first marriage dissolved.

Frankie, born Sarah Francis Clanton, grew up in Shelbyville. She dropped out of high school to work at the pencil mill in order to help with the family finances. There she met the semi-pro baseball player she would later marry, over the strong objections of her parents. Leonard Roberts was handsome, with his black hair and the beautiful smile that his daughter inherited.

When Frankie and Lenny married in 1940, she crossed the Tennessee state line for the first time in her life. They lived with his mother in Brooklyn, New York, until Frankie became pregnant; and then she went home to Shelbyville, where Lois was born on October 2, 1941.

Frankie found out that her husband was not Leonard Roberts, but Leonard Roth and he was AWOL from the service when he rejoined the army December 9, 1941, driven by a patriotic duty unleashed December 7. As a ranger in the Philippines, he was awarded a Bronze Star for valor in Leyte. Frankie also found out Lenny had been married before.

Lenny's mother Irene, using the stage name Dolly Stewart, had been in vaudeville with her husband, playing the Shubert Circuit. For twenty-five years, Roth and Stewart were headliners with a comic act in which Dolly played the straight man. Lenny traveled with them until he was school age, and then he became a boarding school student.

After her husband's death, Irene remarried and eventually became a motel owner in Winter Park, Florida. There she claimed to be a Methodist from New York, but as Lois discovered when she was almost grown, Nana was actually Jewish and from Hungary.

Lois loved staying with Nana and Grandpa Joe. There, at age three, she met her father for the first time, but as the war ended, so did Frankie and Lenny's marriage.

Lois loved Shelbyville and the Butler's farm. She was outdoors most of the time. "I am Sheba, Queen of the Jungle," she would shout as she ran through the tall grass. And she knew she could fly. All she had to do was be high enough and she could take off. She strongly felt this to be true, although she never really tried.

The Butlers considered themselves her adopted grandparents. "I'll help hunt for eggs," she told Mrs. Butler and skipped down the path to the hen house with the egg basket. "I'll help milk," she told Mr. Butler and sat on the small stool pulling at the cow's teats with her small hands, trying to fill the molasses bucket Mrs. Butler had cleaned just for her. She felt loved and secure. Lois was always thankful for the Butlers and their farm.

At this time Frankie was being courted by John Pollack, a tall, good looking man who worked at the Goodyear factory.

One day Frankie called Lois to come sit with her on the porch. "I have something important to tell you, dear," she said as she held her daughter's hand. "I am going to marry John. I hope you will like the idea of having our own home again."

"Oh yes, mother," Lois cried, jumping up and dancing around. "And now I will have a daddy just like everyone else." She sat down beside her mother. "Can we have a cow and chickens like we have here?"

"I don't think so dear. We will be living in town, but you might have a pet," her mother said and gave the child a hug.

Frankie and John were married in 1947. She knew he had been married before, but later she found out that theirs was his third marriage. John had been wounded during War II and thought he could not father any children. When their daughter Jean was born, Lois was seven, and the entire family was thrilled with the new baby.

"I'll hold her," the bright-eyed Lois said, and Frankie would place Jean on her small lap. "I love you," Lois would coo and begin to sing. She loved holding her sister—that is until the telephone rang. "I'll get it," Lois would call at the first ring, jumping up without remembering the baby was in her lap. Frankie soon learned to come running if Lois had the baby when the telephone rang.

Three years later Jane was born, but the thrill of having a new baby sister was gone. Lois was now more interested in friends her own age.

Also around this time, Lois lost being the queen of any jungle. It was recess, and Lois had borrowed a friend's bright red sunglasses. Lois felt tall and powerful as she ran though the school yard wearing the dark glasses, but the sunglasses slipped and fell to the ground. Lois stepped on them and heard them snap beneath her shoe. She stopped running. She was so embarrassed! Her face flamed! She had not meant to break the glasses, and she felt like a klutz. At ten years of age Lois began to have negative thoughts about her abilities.

Soon after Frankie and John were married, he became a state trooper. This meant the small family moved often when he was reassigned or promoted. Lois attended eleven different schools between the first and sixth grades. When John made Sergeant, they settled in Gallatin, Tennessee. Lois now had one group of friends from the seventh grade until she graduated from high school. Police were much respected during this time, so his occupation was not a burden for Lois. But her dates, who had to come to the door to pick her up, were met by a six-foot-four officer in full uniform, complete with holster and gun.

Lois knew she never wanted to be a secretary, so she did not take typing in high school. She did not feel she was capable of going to college for the number of years required to become a teacher either. When she learned about a three-year nursing program, she was elated. After graduation she worked, as a waitress and later as a nurse's aide, to earn enough money to attend the Baptist School of Nursing in Nashville.

When Lois found out she had to take classes at Belmont College, she almost panicked. She tried not to worry and told herself that since the administrators of the program had seen her grades and still accepted her, they must have thought she could do the work. She did well, but really missed her family. She rode a Trailways bus home to Gallatin every Friday night and cried as she rode it back to school on Sunday afternoon.

Her sophomore year she roomed with her best friend in nursing school, Linda Poore. One day the two girls were walking down the hospital corridor. Lois had a bed pan in one hand and a Hershey bar in the other. She was almost in tears as she said, "I can't get anything right. Maybe I should quit even trying."

"Lois, how can you be so down on yourself?" Linda asked. "You handled that last case like a pro. You fed the newborn formula instead of water, but you told the doctor, and he changed the chart for you. The baby is just fine." Linda shook her head, "Your self-esteem is the lowest of anyone I've ever known."

Lois knew she was right; another nursing student and a friend from high school had said the same thing. How can I be this way, she asked herself as she went into the laundry room to collect clean linen for her patient.

Later she told Linda, "I haven't always been like this. Once I was Sheba, Queen of the Jungle. And I just knew I could fly." She told Linda about breaking the sunglasses. Then she remembered a time when she had been assertive. "My friends and I were sitting on a hill above the sidewalk when some kids came by and started bugging us. I stood up and challenged them by shouting 'I bet you can't even spell hemisphere,' a word I had probably just learned to spell myself.

"And there was the time on the playground when I flexed my arms and told some really big boys, 'I'll beat you up,' when they said me and my friends should start behaving."

Linda laughed as she visualized a young Lois threatening anyone.

Lois frowned as she remembered, "Nana had me sing 'Ta Ra Ra Boom Dee Aye,' at the neighborhood bar when I was probably four. I certainly didn't have any problems then."

What has happened to me, she wondered. That night she told Linda, "In Gallatin there were these photographers, Birdie and Tip Crutcher. These wonderful people actually got me to enter a beauty pageant—twice. I was scared to death." Lois smiled at the memory. "They showed me how to walk, carry myself, and apply make-up for the stage."

"No wonder it's so hard to believe you could have this problem," Linda said. "I guess I just know you so well."

Before going to sleep, the two young girls discussed ways Lois could improve this small flaw in her character. Finally Lois said, "I'll just act confident, and it won't show."

Nurses' training changed the way Lois looked at the people around her. When the student nurses were assigned to the mental hospital at Central State for four months, they were frightened. They did not have much knowledge or preparation, and they thought of the patients there as "crazy people."

"We all know about crazy people," Linda said to Lois, "they are locked up."

"Remember what the supervisor said," Lois cautioned. "If you begin to doubt whether you are the patient or the nurse, put your hands in your pocket. If you have the keys, you are the nurse."

One of the first patients Lois saw when they went to the hospital was a girl she had known in high school. One summer they had spent almost every day together. Lois's eyes were opened about mentally ill people. Now, she realized, she had grown up with them; they were her friends, and they were everywhere. Although she said she rattled her keys a lot during that time, she also said, "I am one of them." She no longer saw mental patients as different, but as people with problems and challenges that made some easier to reach than others. She began to see that there were gifts in tragedies, and this insight would be of great help to her all her life.

One night Linda was sitting at the dresser, rolling up her hair, when Lois came into the room. "This week we're going to the Senior Citizens' Center," Lois said and plopped down on her bed.

"It'll be like a nursing home with people so old they just sit around and drool on each other," said Linda.

Lois laughed, "Or they'll be dull people playing chess."

What they saw at the center was people running around everywhere. Yes, there were activities for the elderly, such as quilting, but there was also dancing. Lois was astounded. "This is not slow dancing," she said to Linda. "They are *dancing!*"

She began to realize that people did get older, but they didn't have to get decrepit as they aged. Isn't this a wonderful thing for a twenty year-old to find out, she thought. She now knew if she took care of her body, she could stay active all of her life. This experience always influenced how she dealt with older people. Whenever she worked with them, she tried to get them to exercise.

During her last year in nursing school, Lois began dating a doctor. Paul Green had begun his OB/Gyn practice four years before. After

Lois graduated and had worked a year at Baptist Hospital, she and Paul were married.

The prestige of being a doctor's wife did help the new bride's self-esteem. Lois thought it was through the power of people that she regained her lost self-esteem. She credited friends like Marie Maxwell and Patricia McPherson. "They," she said, "helped shore me up." Marie always gave her positive compliments, and Trish was president of every group she joined and gave her responsible jobs to do. And probably Lois herself, and her way of looking for the positive in any situation, helped bring about the change.

Lois believed the fact that she had lost and regained her self-esteem was important. Years later she would use her experience to hold workshops on the subject. "It is important that you know," she told those who attended her lectures, "that I lost my own self-esteem around the fifth grade, but I regained it before I was 30."

After their marriage, Paul and Lois moved to Huntsville, Alabama, where he hoped to have a larger practice with a new partner. They soon found that they missed Nashville and their friends, so they moved back home after being in Huntsville less than a year.

As a doctor's wife, Lois had quit working and had begun the volunteer work that would eventually change her life. At first she joined other doctors' wives, participating in such matters as public relations, fund raising, or volunteer recruitment for the Huntsville Symphony Guild, and later the Nashville Guild and Nashville Academy Theater. Lois enjoyed this work, and she was very good at it. Then her mother, Frankie, was diagnosed with colon cancer.

2

It was early 1965 when Frankie first began having pain in her rectal area. Hemorrhoids, she thought, and went about the business of caring for her family. When she began to notice blood whenever she went to the bathroom, she made an appointment with Dr. Johnson.

After an examination and some tests, he advised her that the diagnosis was colon cancer. In nursing classes, Lois knew she had studied this disease, but she could not recall anything about it. She was caught up in the word "cancer" and could only think, How in the world can I live without my mother?

Immediate surgery was required, resulting in a colostomy. Lois sat in the waiting room with her sisters and her stepfather. She stood up when the doctor came to the door.

"I think we got it all," he said and went into the details of Frankie's recovery. "She will be just fine." Dr. Johnson had been the family doctor for many years. He was a wonderful man and trusted by the family. His optimism made them feel better about the scary diagnosis.

"Oh dear," Lois said to Paul that night. "Mother must be worried about having a colostomy."

"In what way?" he asked.

"Well, the only person she has ever known with a bag was an elderly woman who lived down the street from us years ago." Lois remembered it vividly. "The poor woman wasn't regulated, smelled, and had to wear the bag all the time."

"I know people who have colostomies, and that is not true of them," Paul said.

They discussed the care that must be taken. "At least I am not repulsed by this," she said.

Lois helped Frankie adjust to the colostomy. "Time to change the 'Rose Bud,'" Frankie would say, and soon she was taking care of it without any help.

After one year, the symptoms returned. Frankie had more surgery, and this time she had to have chemotherapy. She became deathly sick and vomited so much Lois felt her mother actually turned green.

Dr. Johnson admonished the family to try to keep Frankie's spirits up. Lois smiled at that, and the doctor knew it would be no problem for the vivacious daughter. "She doesn't need to know she has cancer and how serious her condition really is," he said. "Just tell her she is doing fine." Lois had doubts about his advice, but she didn't know what else to do.

Lois was thankful for her nursing skills. She was able to give her mother the care that allowed Frankie to leave the hospital and go home.

One day Lois was at her mother's side when Frankie said, "I will be glad when this is over."

"Oh, Mother!" Lois said. "Don't talk like that; you're going to be all right."

"I don't want you children to grieve," she began.

Lois quickly changed the subject. "What do you think you could eat tonight?" Lois asked as she adjusted the pillow under her mother's head. "Do we need to wait for Pop to come home and see what he would like?"

Frankie sighed and said, "You know he won't care what we have."

So she could go home at night, Lois taught Jean and Jane to give their mother shots for pain, but Lois was there when Frankie died on June 10, 1967.

Over the years, Lois thought about this time and how hush-hush anything related to cancer was and how no one talked about dying. Lois knew she was the logical one for Frankie to have talked with about her sisters, but Frankie was not allowed to say the things that only a mother could have said about their future and their welfare. Jean had just graduated from high school, and Jane had just had her sixteenth birthday when they lost their mother.

Lois realized too late that Frankie had died without talking about her issues and concerns. "She did everything except hit me over the head, but I would not let her talk about leaving us," Lois told those she later counseled.

Lois grieved hard and long for her beautiful mother. When she was in nursing school, Lois had often wondered why Frankie had never encouraged her to get more than a high school diploma. Mother just did not realize the importance of an education, she thought. Now she knew her mother had given her an open slate, and she would always say it was because of her mother that she found her true vocation. Lois knew she did not want anyone else to go through the dying process alone. "My mother died in complete isolation, surrounded by people who loved her," she said.

At the age of twenty-six, Lois faced the finality of death. At first she became very angry and turned away from God, but she did see how very precious life was and became determined to live hers as fully and completely as she was able.

After Frankie's passing, Lois tried to contact her father. Through Army records, she found that he too had died. The cause of death was lung cancer.

3

After eight years of marriage, Lois and Paul became the proud parents of a beautiful baby boy. Paul Arnold Green III was born April 27, 1972. For the birth certificate, Lois legally changed her hated name to Lois Ann.

When Lois's half-sister Jean was born, John Pollack had stopped his wife from having any further contact with her ex-mother-in-law. However, Lois's grandmother Nana did get in touch with Lois soon after Frankie died.

Nana came for a few days, but did not show any sympathy. She only made derogatory remarks about Frankie. The grief was too raw, so Lois wrote her grandmother, saying how much pain that visit had caused her. They became estranged, but after the birth of her son Lois felt a need for him to be connected with his great-grandmother. She wrote Nana and told her about Paul III. Nana did not respond, but Lois continued to write. Nana finally answered and saw Paul III when he was four, but she had not seen Lenny, her own son, for 15 years.

Although Nana did not mention Frankie again, Lois realized that Lenny Roth was perfect in his mother's eyes, so she could not fault him for the divorce. She had to blame someone else. It was Lois who told Nana that her son had died, but Lois always felt that her beloved grandmother had known, somewhere in her mother's heart, that this was so.

As Paul III got older and began attending Oak Hill School, Lois volunteered her services at the school. She also remained active in programs involving the cultural aspects of Nashville. Then she began seeing articles about Hospice in the local paper, and it brought back the agony surrounding her mother's death. So in 1978 she volunteered with Alive Hospice. She became involved with counseling individuals who were facing terminal illnesses and their families. She found that the general public did not accept the idea of Hospice. Since people did not talk about cancer, they certainly were not going to talk about death.

At first Alive Hospice had no social workers or nurses, so Lois, as a nurse, was very welcome. Some of those first volunteers might be called sandaled-hippies, but Lois, drawn by their dedication, felt no difference. Together, they learned to listen and counsel. Lois also helped see that physical needs were met by arranging for hospital beds, wheel chairs, or walkers. Later, as a board member, she co-chaired fundraising events.

One Monday afternoon, Lois was on the telephone talking with a bereaved mother. As soon as she hung up, she went to the office of staff psychologist, Billy Thomson. "Billy," she said, "I just got off the phone with a mother who lost her premature son two years ago."

She continued to tell Billy the young mother's story. "The baby was born at a local hospital, and the family gave them the body. Mary was adopted, so this baby was her only flesh and blood, and she feels so responsible for his death.

"She blames herself because the doctor had cautioned her about eating salty things, and she got up in the middle of the night to eat a snack of crackers and sardines.

"I made an appointment for Mary and her husband to come in Friday at 2:30," she said. "I was hoping you might be here, too."

Billy checked his calendar. "I'm free," he said.

Lois went back to her office. She sat behind the desk thinking about Mary. She wanted to do something—but what? She remembered from her nursing days that hospitals kept some bodies and body parts for a long time. She called a pathologist associated with Hospice, and he gave her the right department. She called the lab.

When the answer came back, "The baby is still here," Lois sat very still. *What in the world have I gotten myself into?* she wondered. She went to Billy and told him what she had done.

"Call back and find out when we can go see the baby," he said, and Lois called the hospital to make the necessary arrangements. Before the counseling session they went to the hospital and saw the baby in the jar of formaldehyde. Lois had never seen a dead baby before. "This is just horrible," she said, "just horrible. I wish I had never called."

"But we must tell the family and let them decide what to do," Billy said, "and it really isn't that bad."

On Friday the family was told about their child. Lois told them exactly how she felt, but the parents still wanted to see their baby.

Lois called the hospital chaplain and asked him if they could use the chapel for the viewing. The mother brought a basket and a blanket. The lab staff wrapped the baby in the blanket and laid it in the basket. They took the baby to his mother and father.

They were in the chapel for such a long time that Lois became anxious, but she tried not to show it. She wanted to be supportive of Billy, who was not worried at all. But Mary may have fainted, Lois thought, and hit her head on a pew. Lois was very relieved when the door finally opened.

"Thank you so much," the mother said, tears in her eyes.

Lois followed the couple down the hall. She was amazed as she saw the mother literally walking on air. Lois was impressed and changed.

"She held her baby and said everything she needed to say," Lois told Billy after the family had gone. "What book did you get that from?" she asked, thinking he could refer her to some text.

"That is not in a book," he said and laughed.

What powerful stuff! Lois thought. She had found out what grieving parents needed. No matter how gross the anatomy or malformations, parents need to be given a choice, then encouraged, not pushed, to do what they feel in their hearts.

Again, Lois felt a tremendous need to help people with the dying process. Nursing dealt with healing people and had not helped prepare her for the needs of the community. Lois decided she must go back to school and get a degree in Social Work.

She began talking to her friends about her goal.

"Go back to school?" one asked as they sat by the pool at the Seven Hills Golf Club, watching their sons swim. "Why would you do that?"

"You are a mature person. You've been to school," said another.

"You have a son and don't need to be working," said still another.

Lois was shocked. This was not a destructive or negative thing she was thinking about doing. This was a positive thing, she thought, to educate myself and do work that was important, and here are people willing to stop me. At the age of thirty-five, Lois had her eyes opened. She learned that the more she trusted herself, the more excited she became about living. Later, she realized that being aware and free to be herself made those she counseled freer to be themselves. If a thing was a truth for her, it didn't matter how many people disagreed. She enrolled at Tennessee State University to get her Bachelor of Science degree in Social Work.

Lois chose TSU because it was affordable; she did not want to put a strain on the family finances. Also, it was the only accredited social work school in the area. Lois had always thought she did not have what it took to be successful in the academic world. So after she applied to TSU and was tested, she called to find out her IQ. She was relieved to find it was reasonably high, and this gave her the confidence to proceed. Actually, it was well above average.

Since she entered college off-schedule, her first class was the second half of American History. She was the only white student and the oldest in the class, including the instructor. When the first class assignment was to write a paper, she was anxious because she felt she did not write well; when she found out she had to present her paper to the class, she was devastated.

Before class she went to the professor. "Dr. Travis," she said, "I am just horrified. I don't know if I can live through this."

Dr. Travis looked at her very nervous new student sympathetically and said, "I'll handle it."

When it was Lois's turn, Dr. Travis announced to the class, "Mrs. Green is scared to death to speak and may not make it through her speech." She looked at the back row where the football players sat together. "Would you men be acutely aware of Mrs. Green, and if she should faint, run forward and keep her from hitting the floor?"

Everyone laughed, and Lois went to the front of the room to begin reading her paper. Lois was surprised at what Dr. Travis had said, but really felt that her professor was being kind. She said what I would have left unspoken, and now I don't have to worry because everyone knows I'm scared, she thought. If I shake like a leaf, it won't matter.

Lois had led small groups on breast cancer, but that was sitting down and very informal. Because she had something really important to say, it kept her going. When she began educating in the community, she was nervous but always had what she wanted to say written out on cards. She had even done spots on radio and TV and felt she was getting better, but presenting her paper in that first history class was the beginning of getting over her fear of public speaking. Years later she called herself a "ham" when it came to speaking.

About the middle of the semester, Lois learned that she should sit in the front of the classroom, because she was so easily distracted by bobbing heads or people talking about other things. She also made it a point to read the schedule and go to meet the teachers whose classes she thought she would like to take and ask permission to sit in on their lectures. She didn't realize that using that time and energy to select a teacher pegged her as being bright.

Going to TSU was more than an academic learning experience for Lois.

Lois: **"Until you have been a member of a minority group, you really don't understand what it means. Being on this huge predominately African-American campus and seeing very few white folks and not having my own group was a different experience, but being accepted from the very first by most of my classmates made** me think about what it would be like if it were reversed. I wondered if my group would be as open to a minority student. Not everyone at TSU accepted me, but enough so that I did not feel uncomfortable on campus, even in that very first history class. There were people, including those football players, who gave me looks that led me to think they were wondering why 'Whitey' chose their school. I understood why they felt that way. I had seen the treatment they had gotten from my majority world. I also saw people whom I felt were saying, 'M'mm, she's got guts. She is the only *Whitey* here who has said good morning or good afternoon to me.'

"After I finished up the basic courses and took more and more social work classes that were housed in one building, I immediately became closer to the students I saw over and over. I participated in school activities and was treasurer of the Social Work club. I was even invited to represent them and run for homecoming queen. I was certainly honored, but I told them my time was past and I was here to get an education. 'This is the time for you youngsters to get those honors,' I told them. I did help make a float for the homecoming parade, rode on it, and threw candy to the crowd.

"To see these people who had been so persecuted in my white world open up their hearts to me made a profound impression on my life. I feel so strongly about racism and know God is working through me. I was not a racist by hating, but by training. I was carefully taught by my family, school, church, community, and even my government that 'separate but equal' was fair. It affected me. I was deprived of having African-Americans as friends, and I know my life was poorer, because now it is so much richer. I look at the strong influence they have been in my life and the love I now have in my life and I am so grateful for the opportunity to change my way of thinking.

"I sadly remember the time I had been shopping in a downtown department store many years ago. I was there in my white gloves with my handbag on my wrist. The white sales woman looked up. She was helping a black woman, who I thought was about my mother's age, and the young girl with her. They were well-dressed, neat, and clean. The clerk stopped what she was doing and said, 'I'll be with you girls in a minute; I need to take care of this lady first.'

"They were being told they had to step aside for this younger woman. I felt a sense of shame that I was afforded that position. I will always regret this incident and that I did not open my 'lily white' mouth.

"I also remember a time in my psychiatric nursing days when I had a black patient. The family was very upset and they were loud and troublesome. I had seen many white people doing the same thing, so I did not make a distinction. I felt that their complaints should be treated no differently. One of the nurses said, 'You shouldn't have to put up with that from their kind.' I knew she could not give good care to a patient if she put the family in a different category than herself. To me, she completely lost her humanity, as well as her professionalism.

"I knew that it was through ignorance that I did not speak out as a teenager, but as soon as I was enlightened, I felt responsible. I intend to speak out as long as I am alive on issues such as affirmative action. I personally believe it is necessary to keep this law in place until we are all even.

"In counseling, I don't say to people who have had a trauma in their life that since we have done some work, they should be healed. I ask them. So although there have been changes, we cannot make the determination about racism being in the past for African-Americans. We have to ask them.

"I recently saw on television a highly educated African-American woman being interviewed after accepting a position as president of a prestigious Ivy League college. When asked, she said she still experienced racism almost every day, and she gave an example. Every time she went to a certain department store she was followed, because they believe if you are black you may pick up things that do not belong to you. I don't believe she was making untrue statements to keep up empathy. I am sure she wished she could have said she had not experienced racism in years.

"White people want to say that is behind us, but when this woman says she experiences racism every day, I know they are not listening to the people in those dark skins who are having the experience. I do believe the store did call and apologize after the story was aired.

"The big thing I learned at TSU was that in spite of the injustice that still continues, when reversed, African-Americans open up in pretty good numbers to loving and accepting us. They treat us like we are one of them. That is exactly what happened to me, and that was a beautiful experience.

"Growing up in the south, one learns to categorize people by the way they dress and talk. We may be a little off, but can pretty well tell the sharecropper tenant farmer from the Belle Meade matron. Most white people cannot categorize African-Americans, because they have had such little exposure. At TSU, I learned to tell by voice or dress if somebody was angry or pretty open and accepting. This experience enlarged my community. I could read about something going on in the black community and attend, feeling comfortable, whether it was at Fisk University, Meharry Medical College, or TSU.

"I wanted to open myself to African-American churches. I had a church home with a pastor who was African-American, but when he left I did attend an AME church. I received a warm reception and felt that it was a welcoming home.

"I found an enthusiasm for their music and their speaking with the mouth and the body. It was such a joyous celebration—quite different from my quiet church. We don't get juiced up, but they had drums and other instruments. As they were pounding and jagging, you could feel the energy in the room. I was so glad to have been there.

"I also went to a summer workshop on racism, where I got a new perspective. I heard things from radical speakers that hurt, but they were not speaking about me, but about other people who share my color.

"I have such pride in the African-Americans. We did our best to keep them down, but they have survived. When you get to know another culture which has a different way of looking at things, you grow very rich, and I would not have missed that for the world. I was at the heart of TSU and got to know her people so deeply. Being accepted led to a love for my brother and sister that I wouldn't have had without that experience."

For four years, Lois attended school part-time, but finding out that the college was having funding problems and afraid her program might be canceled, she accelerated her plans to graduate. During these years, she also attended every workshop and professional seminar available. She would call, tell them she was a student, and often was able to attend free.

Lois always had a high energy level, but as her schedule increased, she knew she must take care of herself. She joined a yoga class and looked for a place to walk or jog. She found Radnor Lake.

It was there that Lois celebrated her best Thanksgiving. She asked her son, and then her husband, "Do you really need a bird? Does it mean that much to you?" When each told her it did not matter what they ate, she put meat, potatoes, carrots, and onions in the Crock Pot and went to Radnor Lake. So Lois had a wonderful walk in the woods, enjoying the weather, the trees, and the birds, then came home to a house filled with the delicious aroma of beef stew. Her family got a nutritious home cooked meal, and she had very little cleaning up to do.

"I have been liberated," she told Ruth, a Radnor Lake volunteer she had met. "I will do this for every holiday meal."

Ruth became an important part of Lois's learning experience as she followed her vocation. "She is a gift Radnor has given me," Lois often said.

It was during this time that Lois realized that her marriage to Paul was dissolving. They both had friends who wondered how the two of them ever got together in the first place, and the incompatibility was taking its toll on Lois.

Lois had long believed if there was a problem that could not be solved, she should seek help, so she and Paul went to a marriage counselor. Lois took her role as "wife" very seriously, but found it foreign to who she was. She knew Paul had not done this to her; she had done it to herself. In her mind and by her actions, she made Paul the bad guy, and she did not like the person she was becoming.

Then Nana called to tell Lois she had cancer. There were tumors in her abdomen and her doctor recommended palliative surgery to help her be more comfortable. Nana survived the surgery, but in the recovery room she turned sour and died. Nana remembered her granddaughter in her will, and this money made Lois feel independent enough to plan an end to her marriage.

Although Lois was relieved by her decision, she still had a sense of failure and was concerned for her son. She thought about Paul III as she walked at Radnor Lake, sometimes going five times in one day. She knew she had made a firm commitment to God, but also knew she and Paul were in a stifling marriage that did not benefit either one of them. She needed out.

When Paul asked that the divorce be put off for a year as it would be beneficial in some financial way, Lois agreed. "But," she said, "the marriage has ended, and I want to date. I will be very discreet and hope you will not feel I am cheating and use that against me in the divorce. I have been faithful to you, but now it is just a business arrangement."

Paul realized this was true, and they lived separately—under the same roof—for the rest of the year.

Lois's next goal was to get a Master's degree in Social Work. She planned to go into private practice, and with that degree her clients could file and have the fee paid by insurance.

4

After graduation from TSU, Lois applied and was accepted at the University of Tennessee School of Social Work in Nashville. Her self-esteem was building and she was ready to learn. She attended for six weeks. "The most horrible six weeks of my life," she said. Their method of teaching was foreign to her. According to the professors, she had no problems academically; but when counseling, she did not sit right, leaned forward when she shouldn't, crossed her arms, and showed extremely bad body language. They found nothing right about her.

Lois knew she had a gift for relating to people. She was told she had superior counseling skills by her faculty advisor at TSU. Another professor called her skills "profound" and said it was obvious that she cared about her clients.

Her field placement during her undergraduate studies had been with Michael DeAndrea at the Meharry Community Mental Health Center. Michael was an extraordinary counselor. He orchestrated the group like a conductor as he showed love and respect for his patients. Lois learned from him. She accepted her clients, cared about them, and prized their uniqueness. She knew that when a person was understood, they felt normal. If accepted, they could love themselves and value their preciousness. She began what became the main focus of her counseling. She called it "working from the strength perspective." Many times she found within the clients themselves the resources necessary for self-understanding and for altering basic attitudes.

When Michael was absent, Lois conducted the group by herself. She knew the patients could "eat her alive," but they carefully watched each other and took care of her. Lois knew this was because she always treated the group members with love and respect and did not try to impose her will or opinions on them. When she volunteered to work there another semester, she was welcomed, and it gave her more confidence in her abilities.

In graduate school, for the first time in her life Lois begin to have panic attacks and she dropped out of the UT School of Social Work. She continued working with Alive Hospice, joined the Council on Human Sexuality, and got involved with Nashville Cares—a group dealing with AIDS. She also took a refresher course at the Nashville State Technical Institute to renew her nursing license in order to become a psychiatric nurse.

Then Lois went for her yearly physical. When the doctor found a suspicious lump, she had her first mammogram at the age of forty-six. The doctor called with the results. When Paul answered the telephone, she became distressed, but did understand it was just two doctors talking to each other, even if they were talking about her. Paul handed her the telephone. "It looks serious," he said. Lois spoke to the doctor, then she and Paul discussed the impending surgery. "We can put off the divorce and stay married forever," Paul said.

Lois was quiet for a few minutes. "I appreciate your concern, but no, that is not possible."

After a biopsy confirmed the diagnosis, Lois was overwhelmed. How could this be in my body and I was not aware of it? she asked herself. Here I am healthier than I have been in years, running almost two miles every day, yet I have this disease and may die.

It was a Monday, and Lois was on her way to see a client. Oh dear, she thought as she traveled down Thompson Lane and saw Woodlawn Cemetery on her left. I have cancer, and I am so scared. My son is only fourteen years old; how can I leave him? Tears overflowed.

That evening after yoga class, Lois mentioned her diagnosis to a man she was dating. He immediately told her, "Do not have any surgery, and especially do not have chemo. Just go on the macrobiotic diet; it can cure you."

"That sounds good," Lois said, "but how do you know this?"

"My mother died with this same thing just last year," he answered. "She went though hell. There was surgery and chemotherapy, but it didn't cure her. It was a dreadful experience for everyone!" he finished angrily.

Lois went home thinking what a good idea. She went as far as finding out about the diet, but that was all. For three days she did nothing.

Lois was being up front with her son about the diagnosis and what could be the end result. On the afternoon of the third day, Paul III listened to her talk about not doing anything but changing the way she ate.

"Mother," he said, "if you are not having this surgery because you think you'll be ugly, you don't have a thing to worry about. I saw this program on TV. It was on mastectomies and reconstruction. I'm telling you, they do a pretty good job."

Okay, Lois thought, if this boy with his raging hormones thinks reconstructed breasts look good, they must really look good. "I thank you for telling me this," she said. "You have certainly given me something to think about." Her three-day denial period, as she called it, was now over. Her son had turned her thinking around.

The pressures of school would have prevented her from keeping the doctor's appointment, so Lois felt that what happened at the UT School of Social Work was part of God's plan for her and really saved her life. Through the marriage and impending divorce, she felt she found the strength to have the mastectomy.

Lois thought she had the most phenomenal luck. Malcolm Lewis was her doctor, and he was so knowledgeable.

"First thing we are going to do is get rid of this cancer," Dr. Lewis said after the examination, "but you are young enough to be interested in reconstructive surgery."

Lois made an appointment with Pat Maxwell, the plastic surgeon Dr. Lewis recommended

After a thorough examination, Dr. Maxwell told Lois she was a perfect candidate for a tummy tuck. She left his office thinking, Isn't God wonderful? I have cancer, am going to be all right, get a new breast, and also a flat tummy. What a wonderful gift!

When she returned to see Dr. Lewis, he said, "I want you to think about that surgery." He pushed back his chair, looked her in the eye and continued. "Women are supposed to have soft tummies. Do you really want to have an ironing board for a tummy?"

"Well," Lois said, "I always thought so. That's why I've been running and exercising, but what do you really think?"

Dr. Lewis cleared his throat and looked down at the folder in his hand. "Forbid you should ever have a recurrence," he said and looked at Lois. "I want you to consider an implant. This is a big surgery, and you have only one stomach and two breasts."

What wonderful advice, Lois thought, not only as a doctor, but being a man and saying are you sure that is what you want to do. Lois thought about it and found out as much as she could about the procedure. When she had her mastectomy, she had reconstruction surgery with an implant at the same time. She left the operating room with the beginning of a new breast—a psychologically important event.

During her hospital stay, Lois had many visitors. Through her volunteer work, there were many attractive gay men in her life, and they came to the hospital in droves. They were very kind as they massaged her feet and even peeled grapes for her. Lois knew the nurses thought it quite odd that this older woman was being visited by so many handsome young men.

Lois left the hospital angry with the medical community. She had a wonderful surgeon, support for the surgery, and a prediction of a long life, but during her post-operative care, not a single nurse mentioned that she had lost a breast. There was no support from an emotional aspect. It was treated as if it was not an issue. This seemed phenomenal to Lois. As a nurse and social worker, she knew how important body parts were to people, and nobody was talking to her about her loss.

She knew how lucky it was to have such wonderful friends—both male and female—who made it possible for her to talk about what she was feeling and be supported. She knew most women did not have this because their friends wouldn't let them talk about losing a breast. Trying to be positive, they often said, "You are going to be just fine; you are going to have a long life, and how dare you worry about the loss of a breast?" Dealing with cancer had given her new insight. She began to see the positive beyond the negative. She felt she had gained considerable knowledge to pass on to other women. In her private practice as a nurse counselor, Lois began a mastectomy support group.

Lois: "On the subject of the breast, I know what women are thinking about and what nobody else is talking about. I know most people think the breast is not important, that life is what's important. I have never met a woman, although they may exist, whose breast was more important than her life. They want to live—I want to live—so we are willing to let our breast go, but few of us let it go easily.

"What I realized, as I did more research and study on this issue, was that women have mixed feelings about their breasts, and it goes back to the time when they were little girls. We learn about our bodies and get to know them by touch. During play when we get hit by a ball or when we take a bath, we may be pleasuring ourselves, either by accident or by choice. Clothes are made with darts that emphasize the breasts, and society focuses on the breasts of a woman as if this places a value on who a woman is.

"Mothers have another idea about the breast. Babies are breast fed, and even if a woman does not breast feed, we automatically tend to pull people to our breasts to comfort them. Most women or girls feel their breasts are too small or too large. One may even be larger than the other, and we never seem to be satisfied with the size of our breasts. In our teens, if they are too large we get kidded. Then there are the teenage years and intimacy. Do you let somebody touch them or don't let somebody touch them, and there is the pleasure and the fear that gives. Then you get into a committed relationship, and the place the breast has in intimacy or intercourse is pretty significant. The more arousal by the touch of the breast, the more significant the loss.

"Once, when working with a woman who had had a mastectomy, I thought, if this happens to me, I will have both breasts removed—just be flat, and not worry about it. Well, when it did happen I realized how much pleasure having breasts gave me, both sexually and as a woman. I also realized that without one breast I would be very lopsided, and it was going to be a constant reminder of what I had lost. Here I was, a very active person, and what was I going to do with this empty space? I could put in a falsie that could jump out and dislodge, and I know that most women do not wear their prosthesis at home. If their breasts are any size at all they can get imbalances in the body. Nobody ever talks about that. This is another reason for a woman to consider reconstruction. I do not believe any woman should go through that surgery unless she wants to, but she cannot make a decision unless she has all the information.

"The breast is significant in a woman's life. When you add *Playboy* and its fascination with the female anatomy, then tell a woman she is going to lose a part of her and it is nothing, that's crazy. We do not define ourselves by our breasts and will gladly give them up to save our lives, but it would be easier to give them up if people would recognize we are giving up something.

"I know what was true of me. I found myself discreetly holding my breast when I was out in public. I went to the grocery thinking, this is the last time I will be shopping with my breast. I went to a movie thinking, this will be the last time I take my breast to a movie. Then when I showered and washed my breast for the last time before surgery, it was just like grieving any loss. This was a very, very sad time. Most women have never been given a chance to feel this way, and that is part of the baggage that is dumped on them.

"I encourage a woman who has breast cancer to have a healing session about the loss of a breast. She should ask her women friends in, and it may not be a ceremony but just a gathering so she can talk. If there is a man in her life, he should be included. He can't win. If he acts as if nothing is happening, she wonders how he can *not* notice the loss of this significant body part. If he wants her physically, she thinks, I am in grief here, how can he possibly be interested in sex? And if he doesn't want to be intimate, this needs to be talked about so they can go through it together.

"I have seen women traumatized because they only have a blob of skin with a nipple on it. Breasts need to match. I know I would not like to have to use a form in a bra so my breasts would look the same after reconstruction. Today I would encourage women who are considering tummy tuck surgery to have an implant, and if the cancer reoccurs, then they can have that surgery for both breasts. The advantage in using your own fat and muscle is that it gains weight if you gain weight, loses weight if you lose weight, and the breast is soft. As new techniques are being developed, women certainly need to be informed so they can make a choice.

"But something as simple as 'I'm sorry you've lost a breast' will let her talk about what she is feeling, enable her to cry about it, grieve appropriately, and then go on with her life."

Soon after surgery, Lois headed for her beloved Radnor Lake. She was walking on the Gainer Ridge trail when a butterfly flew in front of her. How colorful it is! She marveled as it landed on a bush nearby. When she moved closer and really looked, she saw that part of its wing was missing. Her immediate reaction was, how sad! Here was this butterfly, so beautiful in flight and in color, yet part of it was missing. Lois began to smile. Isn't God wonderful? she thought. He is telling me that everything is fine. I am still a wonderful work of God, even if my new breast doesn't look anything like the old one. She finished her walk, truly thankful for this blessing. Now over the fear of death and the loss of an important body part, she had the gift of life, and everything from that day forward was precious.

Lois knew she did not have to be in court the day her divorce was final, but she had been there for the marriage and needed to be there for the end. She dressed, "as kicky as I could," she said. She felt she was paying tribute to the marriage, even though she was glad it was ending.

Afterward, she went home, changed, and headed for Radnor Lake. She was looking for the path she usually took when suddenly she thought, why do I feel a need to find a path? I can make it just fine anywhere at Radnor Lake and not get lost. Then she realized she could blaze her own trail if needed. I will be fine on my own, she thought. What gifts this place has given me!

5

Before her surgery, Lois had become part of another group that would help her in her personal commitment of being of service. She had returned to nursing as a psychiatric nurse, working at the Vanderbilt Child and Adolescent Psychiatric Hospital, and later at the Parthenon Pavilion. This was the time of the AIDS outbreak. Lois went to the minister of the Metropolitan Community Church, a gay church, and asked "Do you need someone like me?"

"Oh, yes!" the minister said as tears formed in her eyes. "Oh my, yes!"

Lois did not feel qualified to work with the patients, but she wanted to work with the parents who were finding out that their sons were gay at the same time they found out these sons were dying with AIDS. Actually she was needed to work with both the patients and their families.

From her nursing background she knew how AIDS spread, but she checked with her knowledgeable Paul to be sure. He concurred that it could only be spread with an exchange of body fluids, so she was able to go in, hug, and hold the hands of the dying young men. This was when most members of the hospital staff were covering up and wearing masks. Some went so far as to place a patient's meal tray on the floor outside the room so as not to go near anyone with AIDS.

Lois began by doing histories to get the patients the help they needed. She went into the hospitals and met many who generally died within two months of diagnosis because they did not know the symptoms and did not get help sooner.

It was Valentine's Day and at the request of his sister Jean, Lois went to see Mitchell, an AIDS victim. When Lois walked in, the young man was out from under the covers. His legs were terribly swollen. Lois went to the nurses' station, got some scissors, and slit the legs of his pajamas. She began touching his legs and massaging his feet ever so gently and lovingly. She took him through a meditation, using deep breathing, and taught him to connect with the Divine by resting in the white light.

"Close your eyes," she said. "Try to see a pinpoint of light coming toward you. As it gets closer, it gets larger, like the light from an oncoming train. Take a deep breath," she continued, "and feel warm and safe in your cocoon of light."

Mitchell kept his eyes closed as Lois ministered to his legs and feet. She stopped and put her hand on his shoulder.

"Lois," he said looking up and giving her a weak smile, "you have such pretty hair."

Lois patted his hand. "Thank you, kind sir," she said and laughed.

Very hesitantly, Mitchell asked, "Would you do my funeral?"

Lois was astounded at the request. She could barely answer. "I am so flattered that you would ask this of me, so please let me think about it." She knew his family belonged to a denomination that would conduct a certain service and it would not be appropriate for her to say "yes," but Lois did read from the *Illuminata* at his funeral.

As Lois was leaving the room, Jean told her how Mitchell could not stand to be touched. "His legs and feet have been so tender no one has been able to touch him for days until now. Thank you, Lois," she said and hugged her friend.

Lois walked to her car feeling most grateful for having been with this young man. *Just instinctively knowing I could touch him is holy work,* she thought, and she felt her heart open up.

The next day she went to interview for the Mental Health Co-op.

"This is the longest resumé I have ever seen," the Personnel Director said. When he saw the BS in Social Work, he said, "You need your masters in Social Work. You should really think about it."

"Well," Lois hesitated, "I might as well tell you, I had a bad experience at the UT Graduate School and did not feel I could continue."

"Oh, we have a woman working here who goes to school in Louisville. Her name is Teresa Ingram, and you should talk to her."

"I knew Teresa at Parthenon Pavilion," Lois said and smiled.

After the interview, she went immediately to Teresa's office. She listened intently as she told her about the Kent School of Social Work.

"Lois," Teresa said, "they will treat you like an adult."

"*Ping*." Lois heard.

"You'll like it there. They will respect you as the professional you are."

"*Ping, ping*," she heard.

As Teresa talked, Lois noticed a pink aura surrounding her, and then Teresa. The *pings* she heard were very real, but she knew they were in her mind and her awareness. She did not hear them with her ears; she felt them. Her path was clear; she was going to Kent.

"I know this school is where I need to be," she told Teresa. "*Ping, ping, ping.*"

Reaching home, she called the school and asked if there was an opening.

"There is an opening, but it's too late for your application and references to get here before March 1," she was told. It was February 15, but Lois knew from the experience in Teresa's office that the time frame did not matter. She got everything together in seven days, went to Louisville and put them on the proper desk. She soon had the call saying she would be starting school in September, 1995.

6

Another gift from Radnor Lake, Lois always said, was Wayne Palmer. She had talked with Wayne and Jeff Sinks, his boss, many times. In fact, although she was dating other men, she claimed she shook her hips and batted her eyes at Wayne, but from his response she had decided he was not interested in her.

One of the men Lois dated was interested in canoeing. One weekend he was going to a white-water rafting school and asked her to go along. Most of the participants were interested in learning this sport, but Lois was not. She just enjoyed being in the sun and playing in the water. Her fellow rafters conspired to see she was in the river more than she was in the raft—so much so that she had bruises over every extremity.

The next time she was walking at Radnor Lake, Wayne stopped her. "Haven't seen you around in a while," he said.

Lois showed him her bruises. "I went to white-water rafting school," she said.

When Wayne said, "I need to take you canoeing," she immediately pinned him down.

"What day?" she asked.

When they went canoeing, Wayne had on his bathing suit. Lois had not realized how muscular he was. When she took off her blouse and shorts, she thought, what made me think I could date this man? Here she was in a ten-year-old tank suit with her forty year-old body doing what bodies do, and he was eleven years younger and in the prime of his life.

Years later he told her it was one of the prettiest suits he had ever seen. He hadn't noticed that it was old-fashioned. It was things like this that made her so comfortable with him.

When Lois began dating after her marriage dissolved, she insisted on paying her own way. She did not want to be beholden to any man, so on her first date with Wayne, she brought a picnic lunch. "Since you are furnishing the canoe, I will furnish the food," she told him. Whenever they went to a movie or ate dinner, she always paid her share. She said, "Wayne had never met a woman who paid for herself," and laughed as she added, "He loved it."

Their relationship evolved slowly. She told him up front she would never marry again, and she was too old to have children. "I will commit and be faithful, but never marry," she said. Wayne had been engaged once, and when it did not work out he was very hurt. He was determined not to get hurt again. Lois was patient, and Wayne's words "fond of you" eventually changed to "I love you."

But there were problems in the relationship. Whenever they had a disagreement, Wayne would leave and "cave." Their periods of separation often lasted three or four weeks. At first she went after him and they talked it out. "Our arguments never seem to get resolved," Lois told Wayne, "because you don't know how to deal with conflict." She suggested they go to couples' counseling. They found two strong therapists: Dave and Dianne. During their visits, the four would talk together and also do one-on-one sessions.

One day while Dianne was with Wayne, Dave said to Lois, "Have you ever been with a man who just adores you?"

"Why would a woman choose to be with any man who didn't?" Lois replied. She knew it was a blessing that Wayne adored her. She really felt it was a gift and did not take it lightly. Her definition of "adore" was being cherished, and she knew Wayne realized he had something special in her. And she certainly felt she had something special in him.

Lois loved the way Wayne enjoyed outdoor activities. "He encouraged me to do things I had not done since I was a little kid," she said. They both liked walking in the early morning. When it snowed, they would hurry to make the first footprints at Radnor Lake. When Wayne told her about thermal underwear, she felt he had given her a miracle.

Now she could walk all year long. She liked the fact that he had access to a canoe, and they could spend the day on the Harpath River. She loved this gentle man who stopped to release turtles from trout lines. She never forgot their first trip to Florida. On the Interstate, Wayne came to a screeching halt and went back to get a turtle out of the road.

Lois felt Dianne and Dave were very influential in their relationship, but there were still problems. When she began graduate school she told Wayne, "I am going to have to focus on school for a year, and I will not have time for anything else or anyone else. I'm not going to be able to be much of a partner for you or help in this relationship."

Wayne did not change his schedule around the time she was free, and she confronted him about that. Things did get better for a while, and then they began to have distance again.

At the time of her second diagnosis, they had been apart for months. Lois had tried to show him how to resolve his issues and thought he should have learned from the many other times when she had left him alone.

Without Wayne on Valentine's Day, Lois gave herself a party. She had champagne, lit innumerable candles, and got out all her pictures and school annuals. She was going to celebrate the men who had been in her life. She thought about her father, stepfather, sweethearts, friends, and went over what each had taught her. She thanked both Pauls—her ex-husband and her son—for what they had given her. Even the "octopus" who would not believe her when she said, "No," taught her how to handle situations when she was uncomfortable and had to take a stand. She hoped he had grown up and realized how insulting he had been to her.

She pulled out a picture of a young man she had dated in high school. In fact, his next girlfriend had asked for that picture, saying his mother wanted it. When Lois called Henry's mother and she said, "No, dear, that picture is yours," Lois kept it. One Saturday they had gone to Mongomery Bell State Park to swim. When they arrived, Lois discovered that her period had started and her white shorts were ruined, then her bathing suit zipper broke. A woman gave her some money to get some Kotex and pinned the suit on her. Lois wrapped a towel around herself and went out to the pool where Henry had been waiting and waiting. When he grabbed her hand to pull her into the water, she had to explain why she couldn't go swimming. Henry said his basketball coach had explained about "those things," so she didn't have to go into much detail. He was extremely thoughtful, and Lois blessed that coach. Her mother was appalled that she came home wearing her bathing suit, but after explanations she was very sympathetic.

Lois had heard that Henry was married and living in West Tennessee. When she and Wayne went to Memphis to see Linda, her nursing school roommate who was ill with cancer, Lois found his name in the telephone book. She called and found out from his wife that he had recently died. They talked many times, and Lois told her how special Henry had been and about the miserable date.

"I know I was supposed to connect with his widow because she was grieving." Lois told Wayne, "and I could help her." When they went to Memphis to Linda's funeral, they stopped by to meet Henry's wife and take her the high school picture. "It's amazing the lives we touch," she told Wayne. But on that Valentine's Day, thinking that their relationship was over, she had written Wayne a letter, thanking him for what he had given her.

Later, when she talked about her special evening, she said she thought about the toads as well as the princes, "for I have kissed many toads—many, many toads."

After the doctor confirmed that the cancer had metastasized, Lois began to think how Wayne would feel if he heard about it from someone else. When she was walking at Radnor Lake, she approached him. "There is something you might want to know. I have a more serious problem with this cancer," Lois said and told him the latest diagnosis.

"I want to be with you," Wayne said and reached for her hand. "I want the relationship back."

"There is no relationship," she said. "You couldn't be here when things were good, how can you be with me when things are bad? You need to think about it. This is going to be a hard trip, with ups and downs the likes of which you have not experienced. And if you care, it is going to be painful. I could be dead in two years. Do you want to open the door to that?"

"Yes," he answered. "I most definitely do."

Lois brushed back her hair. "I don't accept that," she said and frowned at him. "You go home and think about it for two weeks. Live with it, and think about it deep and hard."

Wayne came back as a friend. Lois told him, "If you want anything with me, you'll have to earn it. I'm in grad school, dealing with more surgery, and will not have time to work on this relationship. You will have to do it."

Wayne changed his schedule so he could be with Lois whenever she was not in school or having to study. He cooked meals, did laundry, and made Lois's hectic life easier.

Wayne had never known Lois without doctors and surgery. "We have come through some really tough times together," she told him, "and I am stronger because of it."

"My life is so much fuller with you in it," he said.

With the last diagnosis, Lois began to think about her gay friends who were as committed and married as anybody else, but who received no support from society whenever a partner died. Here was Wayne, who had been with her so long and was completely committed to her. Lois had said they would marry on her death bed, but she knew they should not wait. They were married May 20, 2000.

7

Over the years, Lois talked about being gutted three times in her career. "It is horrible when you are accused of professional misconduct, and there is no way you can prove your innocence," she said to Wayne. "So often it becomes a hidden secret."

She had been a psychiatric nurse for two years and she loved it when a new community outreach program, referred to as CAPS, was begun. Lois had appreciated the nurse who was going to head the program, and when she was asked to go to work there she said "yes" immediately. The program required good assessment and communication skills, since they would be dealing with other hospitals in an effort to ease the admittance of patients.

At CAPS, Lois had to be on call a certain number of nights a month, and although she did not get called very often, she began to have health problems. She was such a heavy sleeper that she was afraid she would not hear the telephone ring. She soon found herself unable to sleep. The times when she was on call and missed sleep began to affect her health. She had one cold or virus after another. Since she had had cancer, she knew she dared not compromise her immune system.

Lois told the director what was going on and was told, "You will adjust." Lois continued working, but things were not getting any better. Lois called the Sleep Disorder Clinic at Vanderbilt to get some advice. They explained that some people just cannot do night shifts.

Lois went to the director again and told her what was said. "I will gladly be on call until 11:00 p.m. or until midnight, do twice as many nights as required, and start at 5:00 a.m. I just cannot be on call all night," she said, "or I will have to leave."

The director said, "No, nothing else can be worked out."

Lois got a letter from her doctor and took it to the director, hoping she would accept his recommendation. When she would not, Lois turned in her letter of resignation.

There had been no complaints about her work during the six months Lois had worked there. She had loved the work, and she did it well. On the final day, Lois came in, stopped and talked to some social worker friends before going into her office, and generally was telling everyone good-bye. She knew that if an emergency came up she would certainly deal with it, but mainly she set about closing out her records.

The director came in and literally threw a tantrum. From the time Lois had turned in her resignation, it was obvious the woman had been upset, but there wasn't anything Lois could do about it. That day the woman went on a rampage. She began to demean Lois about the work she had done, about work that wasn't done, and about coming in late. Lois was dumbfounded; this was the first time she had heard any complaints. She had never been put in such a position before. She was humiliated.

Somehow, Lois knew to call Personnel. She really felt this idea was a gift from God as she reached over and picked up the telephone. "I need a witness," she said. "I don't know what has happened, but this is my last day and my supervisor is saying all sorts of things about me that are not true. I need somebody to be a witness."

The lady from personnel said, "An immediate meeting will be called, and I will be glad to be a witness. You can also have a friend be a witness for you."

Lois brought her social work friend, and the personnel director brought the assistant director of the psychiatric hospital. The CAPS director spit out all the venom she felt about Lois.

There was no way Lois could defend herself. "I expect every day to make a mistake and have someone say 'You shouldn't do this or that,' but the gist of what I just heard is all new to me," she said. "And if I worked the next two weeks, I couldn't get caught up on all that she has said needed to be done."

The personnel and psychiatric hospital directors decided how Lois would finish out the day. She was told to make so many telephone calls then hand in her things and go on her way. There was no farewell party; there was no chance to say good-bye to anybody. Lois left, feeling like she was trailing guts out the door.

Lois went home feeling disgraced. This is a small community; I will never work again, she thought. This is work that I love. What will I do? The bottom was torn out of her world. It was terribly traumatic for her.

Three days later, the director of the unit where she had worked two years called. "Lois, I heard what happened. I am so sorry, but I want you to know I have staffed whole units with people who have gone through this same thing. You will heal, you will be stronger for it, and," she added, "you will get another job."

These were the first positive words Lois had heard since the incident. She always said that telephone call helped her survive.

The second time, she was working for Nashville Cares. Lois was hired to do intakes for AIDS patients. "It is a job that God made for me," she said. She used every skill she had. She was good at meeting people and making them comfortable so she could educate them quickly. It was one of the best organizations for AIDS in the country at the time. At first she got along really well with the acting director, but eventually there was some conflict among the staff people. Obviously some did not like her, and his attitude changed. He began doing destructive things, like putting her in an office where there was no privacy while she was doing very private work with her clients. She asked for and got an empty office in the basement. There were two rooms, so Lois planned to use one as a waiting room. As soon as she had her office set up, the acting director placed someone in the other office, so again there was no privacy. He used every opportunity to treat her in a negative way.

One day Lois received a call from a family whose son was a drug addict, had AIDS, and was drinking heavily. There was an unmarried sister and her two children also living in the home. When Lois did an assessment, she found that the son was very ill and maybe had two months to live. She also learned that the father was a recovering alcoholic.

"If I can quit, I know you can," he told his son.

Everything was going smoothly. Lois talked about her spiritual connection as she talked with the young man about his drinking. "Drinking can keep a person from having a good relationship with everyone, including your Maker," she said. "Even though you have this serious disease, this is your chance to clean everything up before you leave." She smiled at the young man and reached for his hand. After much discussion, Lois was delighted when he agreed to go into a rehab program. She stood up and said her usual joke, "Give me a hug before I have to slap you." The young man responded with a smile and returned her hug.

In the interviewing process, Lois found out that the children had been exposed to needles. The grandparents thought they were clean needles, but they were willing to have the children tested in case they had been dirty.

Lois knew this was a case that she might have to report for the safety of the children, and since she worked for the agency, she went to the acting director.

"This family has agreed to have the children tested. Do we need to report it?" she asked.

"Yes," he said, looking up and frowning. "It has to be reported."

"This may cause real problems with the family," Lois said. "The father is an alcoholic, and I am not sure he has had a good recovery." She suggested that they wait, and if testing wasn't done within the week, report it then.

"Oh, no," he said, "it has to be reported, and that is final."

Lois went back to the family. "You told me about the children being exposed. I have talked with my director, and he says I have to report this to the proper authorities. I could not report this behind your back, and I really don't think you will ever have anyone call on you, but I will stand behind you."

The father went berserk and all of his addictive behavior came out. The family left, extremely upset with Lois, and she was afraid the young man would not go into treatment.

Lois immediately went to the acting director and told him what had happened. Then she wrote up everything that had occurred, including his advice, to protect herself.

Two weeks later, she was called into his office. "You have been reported by another agency," he said. "The mother said you had been very abusive to the family. Evidently you told the patient he needed to get right with God before he died, and then you told him you were going to slap him if he didn't hug you."

"I said that after a long session and in jest. I have said that many times, and I felt we knew each other so there would be no misunderstanding."

He continued by telling her that since she had been accused, she would have to be relieved of her duties and would only answer the telephone. "You can see clients, but that will have to be done one-on-one under my supervision," he said.

Lois knew this was not unusual and was done in most agencies, but it was done by therapists who respected each other. Part of what Lois was as a therapist was who she was as a person. She could not discuss therapy without discussing her personal life, and she would not be able to bare her soul with a fellow therapist who had gutted her.

"I cannot do that with you," she said. "I would be very glad to do that with someone whom I could respect and learn from."

"Then I guess you are fired," he said.

Lois said, "No, I will take a leave of absence until we get this cleared up."

There was no one in the organization who was his equal, so Lois went to the board to try to get someone to understand that this was a no-fault firing. Nobody wanted to hear what she had to say. There was a new director coming in, and Lois contacted him. He told her he would look into it when he arrived.

It so happened that soon after this incident, Lois received a letter from a colleague who had just had a similar experience. She was holding a workshop on this very subject. "Like anything else bad that happens to you, it needs to be talked about," the letter said. Lois knew this was a horrible thing to happen to a professional, and it could have become a hidden secret. "It damaged my ability," she said, but by attending the workshop soon after the incident she began to heal more rapidly.

The new director came, and after his investigation pointed out that the acting director should have been the one to tell the family the needle incident was to be reported. The other agency was contacted, and Lois was exonerated from their accusation of abuse. The acting director resigned and left the state. Lois was then offered her job back, but a new position had opened up to her.

She was to be an outpatient consultant with a good salary. The hospital had already changed some rules in order to use her experience in place of the required degree. They hired her with a handshake, but there was one psychologist who said he would not send any patients if Lois got the position, so she lost the job.

When Lois first worked as a psychiatric nurse, there was a social worker who was so protective of her clients she would never let anyone call them out of a session. Whenever this doctor tried to see his patients, Lois was the one to go out and tell him they could not come out of group. "He must have seen me in the role of a demanding mother," she said, "and he hated me." Lois was sorry she lost out on the job, but she laughed over that incident.

These experiences allowed Lois to see the role of a therapist more clearly, and she became more skilled in her counseling.

Lois: **"I believe a gutting is most likely to happen when you have lost the support of a superior. It is not important why it happens,** except that you have been blind-sided and will begin to question everything about yourself. You feel you will never work again and will wonder what is wrong with you.

"We are under the premise that if we do good work and have a good knowledge base, everything will be fine. But you can be absolutely right in your work, and someone can use what you do in a negative way and make you the bad guy.

"And this makes therapy so important. It helps people look at something traumatic in a different way. They begin to realize that it didn't happen to them because they were ugly, and it didn't happen to them because they were stupid, and it didn't happen because something was wrong with them, but because something was wrong with the person who did it to them.

"So many people come into the helping profession with their own unresolved problems. They are looking for a fix, but they don't go to a professional and work through these problems. They find out just enough to keep the rough edges from showing. They still have the same issues inside like everyone has because we are all human.

"I recognized a long time ago that I needed to work on my own stuff or it could impact other people. I became willing to lay my soul open and discuss my issues. There are therapists who have not done enough self-discovery, so they are working from their perspective—not a patient's or client's, or even a fellow worker's.

"I am a therapist who believes you should share appropriately. There are some therapists who believe they need to be a blank slate and never share anything about their personal life. I believe you teach by example. You must know what has been helpful to you before it can be helpful to somebody else. Therapists who feel a lot better after sharing need a support group themselves, but if they are sharing something they are already enlightened about, then they can use themselves as an example.

"Some therapists see a need to remake their patients. I often saw that they only needed help in smoothing down some rough spots. This is referring to everyday people dealing with everyday problems, not serious psychiatric problems. Extensive therapy goes back into the past to see what caused a person to think as he does, and then heal it. Many people cannot go back beyond today's problems, so all that might be necessary is to help them see their hurt in a different light or accept it in a different way.

"I have always taken care of myself to keep from being overloaded. I share with other professionals and they with me. I had a supervisor during my field placement with whom I talked routinely, and there was a professor at TSU. When I knew my marriage was in trouble, I sought a therapist and was very open. When anything pops into my life that I cannot resolve, I seek help.

"I always thought I did not have any right being a therapist unless I was willing to go to a therapist myself. By going to this superior person, which implies they had more knowledge and experience, I became vulnerable. Only then could I understand where my patients and clients were coming from when they saw me.

"Also, therapists are only as good as the patients they have. I can be Lois Green and have knowledge and really good experience to work with a person who has an issue and sees a need to change. I can work with patient A, and changes will be made. I can deal with patient B, who has similar issues, work in a similar way, and see no change. Part of that might be because of a slight difference in the way I relate to these two people, but what generally happens is that the clients who make progress work on their issues and do homework outside of our sessions. Patient B might say 'I can't do that; I can't complete this assignment because it doesn't feel right to me.' Patient A believes in me and the skills I have; B for whatever reason doesn't believe in me or himself. There is also a difference if a person comes to therapy by choice and is not there because it was mandated by law or hospitalization. More often than not, these people will show up, but won't do anything to work on their problems.

"I know there is so much good in people. Some may allow their bad side to take over, but I believe we are put on earth to learn how to love—in spite of warts, worldliness, and whatever work we do."

8

Lois continued to work with AIDS patients. Her heart was broken time after time with these young men. There was one beautiful man she interviewed who would soon be twenty. She planned to visit him on his birthday, but he died one week after she met him.

There was another man she assessed for Nashville Cares. He had been in prison, but was sent home to die. When the interview was over, she hugged him. At his funeral the boy's mother said, smiling through her tears, "Lois, you were the only person to hug him outside of the family."

Then she met Randy Boswell, a young man in his early thirties. Randy spoke five languages and had been doing intelligence work. He was living in California, but came home to Nashville after being diagnosed with AIDS. He had been condemned by his parents' minister, but they did not abandon him.

Randy wanted to promote AIDS awareness, so he permitted the local newspaper, *The Tennessean*, to come in and cover his story.

There was a benefit for Randy at a road house that was frequented by the gay community. Lois planned to go, and Wayne agreed to go with her, but when they got to the parking lot, he hesitated.

"I don't have time to take you home," Lois said. "I'm going to the party."

"Well, if someone makes a pass at me, I'll deck him," he said as he followed her.

Lois laughed. "I'd make a pass at you because I think you're a hunky heterosexual guy, but what makes you think anyone here would be attracted to you?"

Wayne was able to laugh, too.

Randy's father had never been in a gay bar before either. He waved when he saw them and came over to Wayne. "What's a nice guy like you doing in a place like this?" he asked. They laughed as they went over to a table, sat down, and enjoyed the evening. Wayne began to visit Randy, learned to love him, and was there with Lois when Randy died. Knowing Randy changed Wayne's viewpoint on homosexuals.

Lois marched in every gay pride parade. As she and Wayne grew closer in their relationship, he marched too. He was nervous as to what it might do to his job or reputation, but he went with her anyway.

During one parade there seemed to be a problem with an enormous rainbow flag. A girl shouted to Lois, "Come up and get this corner." She did, and kept her mouth shut, afraid someone would find out she was straight and take the honor of carrying this flag away from her. "I have tried to learn everything I can about their struggles," she told Wayne. "This was one of my proudest days."

Lois: **"There is a misconception that all gay people prey on young children, but the statistics are much higher for the straight population. Some gay people are promiscuous. They act out sexually and don't practice safe sex, but I am as appalled by their behavior as I am about straights who have those same values.**

"There was a family who did not know their son was gay. The boy tried to get information from the Internet to see exactly what he was feeling, but he also connected with a minister who was opposed to gays. When the preacher told him it was sinful to feel as he did, he would rot in hell, and would be better off dead, the young man killed himself. The statistics are very high for teenage suicides because of what being gay does to them and their families.

"I have a friend, Steve Davidson, who is like a brother to me. This young man is beautiful and bright. Everything about him is so right, but he told me about putting his hand on the television set and praying with a TV evangelist to be relieved from his feelings. Thank goodness he was able to be with people who showed

him that God made him, loved him, and would continue to love him. To me, gay is not evil; gay is just not being straight. As long as Steve has his belief in God and has good moral values, he will be all right. Now he is an avid speaker on gay and lesbian issues.

"Most straight people don't realize the horrors gays live with. Not long ago, one of the gay organizations was looking for office space. A member called and asked for prices, but when they went to see the property and told the landlord who it was for, the price went up. It seems there is a hidden 'gay tax' that no one talks about.

"The reality is that we are in a country that condemns gays because they are promiscuous, yet they cannot marry legally. In fact, there is no law in my state to prevent someone from being fired because they are gay.

"I believe that gays are created by God, and God doesn't create trash. God made them just the way He/She wanted them to be, and I will be supportive of them. I march in every gay parade to stand up for those who cannot stand up for themselves."

Lois gained more experience on how to be of service during the dying process through a friend she had met at Radnor Lake. Lois and Wayne became members of Ruth's support group after she was diagnosed with lung cancer. Ruth had suffered many emotional traumas in her life and was hostile toward her family, with good reason. She had been sexually abused by an uncle who lived with them, but her parents did not believe her. Especially her mother, who had helped raise this younger brother. When Ruth became ill with rheumatic fever, they considered her a weak person and left her in the hospital alone when she had to be confined for bed rest. They considered her the black sheep of the family.

Ruth became somewhat reclusive and very distrustful of most men. As she grew to adulthood, many problems were not resolved, but she had a professional position that provided her with a certain amount of satisfaction. She chose therapy and labored long years to regain her health, but she had great difficulty believing she was a worthwhile person.

Following the diagnosis of cancer and metastasis, she came face to face with her fears and really connected with her true self. She planned and invited over forty people to a "Hurrah for Me" party. Lois looked around as Ruth mingled with her guests and rejoiced that her friend had found this new strength.

When the cancer refused to stay in remission, Ruth asked her friends to be available when she needed them. They became her support group and decided to call themselves the "Wild Bunch." Wayne had pins made, stating, "I am one of the Wild Bunch," and each one wore it proudly.

Cynthia was one of the "Wild Bunch," and also had had rheumatic fever as a child. The two had become fast friends when they met in the hospital. There were also twins, a brother and sister, Ruth had known from college. The sister often told Lois that she was doing things wrong.

"This is not appropriate," she said, "talking to Ruth about her dying."

"Yes, but I am also telling her how much she means to me, and I am saying everything I want to say. This is loving and caring, so there are no tragedies to dissolve."

As Ruth became weaker and weaker, she was hospitalized. The "Wild Bunch" filled her hospital room with balloons and made her surroundings as pleasant and cheerful as possible. "We are making you a nest," Lois said. They visited often.

It was Ruth's idea to have a "Will Signing," complete with pizza. She made Cynthia her administrator. Then Ruth not only bestowed her worldly possessions on those she loved, but she designed her funeral. She chose to be cremated, picked out *Amazing Grace* and other songs that had special meaning for her, and asked several friends to speak.

Ruth's condition worsened. She was not in a coma, but the doctor gave her little chance of living more than a few days. When Ruth rallied the next day, the "Wild Bunch" gathered at her bedside.

"I have to tell you my experience," Ruth said. She told her friends that she had seen a purple stone which was very large and incredibly beautiful. Inside the stone she saw a precious place of peace and love, and there were children playing everywhere.

"And I saw an old man sitting in my window," she said. "He was very old, but very kind."

"Do you suppose he was an angel?" someone asked.

"Oh, yes," Ruth said. "He had to be."

"How absolutely glorious," Lois said.

When she became weaker and was dying, the nurse wanted to call some of the "Wild Bunch." "No," Ruth said. "Leave them alone; I'm going to go play with the children." A short time later, when the nurse went into the room, she found that Ruth had died.

The nurse then called the friends. When they came, Lois took a balloon and put it on the bed. Together the "Wild Bunch" took all the balloons and covered her body. They told Ruth good-bye and talked about the gift of knowing her as they waited for the ambulance.

Although there was one sister who did visit, Ruth had requested that certain members of her family not be allowed in the hospital. She did not want her parents or the abusive uncle to be at her service or have their names appear in her obituary, but in a last act of abuse, they did not respect her wishes. They had their names put in the newspaper, and they came to the memorial service.

"What are we going to do?" Cynthia asked the group.

"I'm so sure Ruth is now in a place where those things don't matter," Lois said, "that we won't have to do anything."

After Ruth's ashes were laid to rest, Lois spoke. "This precious person was a vessel of love and compassion. She was a blessing to all of us who knew and loved her. In spite of, or perhaps because of all that happened to her, she was a teacher and a guide on life's path."

The twin who felt Lois was wrong in the way she dealt with their dying friend later used the same techniques when her mother was dying. She wrote a long letter, thanking Lois for all she had learned while dealing with Ruth's illness and death. "I was wrong in wanting to encourage and give false hopes by telling her every thing was fine."

9

After Lois was accepted at the Kent School of Social Work in Louisville, Kentucky, she called her minister and explained her good fortune. "This is the first time I have ever felt a need to testify, but God's hand is so visible in what has happened. I need to give thanks."

The minister felt Lois's enthusiasm and reverence. "How wonderful," he said, and before they finished talking asked, "Why don't you do the whole service?" As it turned out, Lois did the early service also.

She was very nervous, but this was something she really wanted to do. She wrote out what she was going to say on neon pink paper. "That will be my lucky color," she told Wayne. And the day of the service, holding the pink sheets gave her courage.

"This is new for me, but I am here to tell you that God and the angels do speak to us, clearly direct us, and set things in motion by paving the way for us." She looked over the congregation. "And having said that and believing it with all my heart, I can't tell you how many times this past year I've questioned why I was even here."

She then told the congregation about her friend Ruth, who bravely faced her own mortality. "This beautiful human being was another truth and miracle who gave us the real gift of how to live and how to prepare for death.

"For thirty-two years I have been a nurse. I began counseling the dying seventeen years ago. Sometimes this is hard for people to understand, especially since I'm so full of life and energy, but when I'm involved with someone who's dying and who's sharing that special time with me, I am down to the basics of life. Possessions, finances, status, and all other worldly things have no meaning," she said. "At the end, we get down to the essence of who we are, and that is the most alive and energizing thing I've ever done. To be connected to realness, to the energy of the human spirit, is a miracle."

She continued by telling about her visit with Mitchell the day before he winged his way to the angels and the light of God. "His memorial service was a testimony to love, with a church full of loving people and a grieving father giving voice to his feelings. Love was everywhere and healing was present. This experience with Mitchell is connected to the next miracle."

She told about leaving graduate school ten years before, the divorce, and dealing with cancer. "I received many gifts and blessings from these experiences," she said, "but I felt limited by my lack of credentials. Not having that piece of paper hampered me over and over.

"I often felt foolish because I could not force myself to go to school. My friends encouraged me, and I told them that I had never had to plan things before, as my life just fell into place. Then they told me that I was older now and I had to be in charge of things. And that's where I was on February 15 when it happened."

She told them about her talk with Teresa, the pink aura, and the *pings*. "I have known since the *pings* that this was my path, and I got my acceptance to Kent last Friday.

"This miracle affirmed my belief in a divine plan for my life, and I know I can trust the plan to manifest."

She ended by admonishing her audience, "Be open to the miracles in your life. Affirm them; give thanks for them. Each moment is precious. God and the angels do speak and clearly direct—especially when we are open to receiving. God Bless!"

Lois left the church, feeling uplifted and thankful. Soon, she would have the credentials she thought she needed in order to be of service.

10

After attending Kent for one month, Lois received a diagnosis that after nine years her breast cancer had returned. She had begun to take life for granted, but now she again focused on living. She never said, "Why me?" but felt since she had the knowledge to deal with it and both of her parents had died with cancer, "Why *not* me?"

In graduate school she received another gift through Jason, her partner in Counseling 101. He was an experienced nurse, still working while going to school, and was the therapist for ten weeks while Lois was the patient. Then they swapped roles.

"I know you have a lot on you with graduate school, but this is what is going on with me," she said and told him briefly about her earlier surgery and what she was facing now. "How comfortable do you feel dealing with this?"

"I have worked many hours with cancer patients and even more since I have been working at Vanderbilt," he said, smiling at the serious young woman with twinkling eyes. "I think I can help with your issues and will do it gladly."

So here was a built-in therapist. She met with him two hours a week, and they focused on the cancer and the loss of her second breast. Lois found that he did have experience, not only with the cancer, but also the emotional issues, and was not just learning, but knew the ropes and could encourage her.

Lois had her second surgery on a Thursday and was back in school on Monday. She felt that she had nothing to worry about for God was watching over her. Since it had been nine years from the first surgery, she had very little fear and focused on graduate school.

Lois had graduated and worked one year when she went to the plastic surgeon for her final visit. "I said something to the nurse about four months ago," she told the doctor as he was finishing the examination, "and we both think it is the edge of the implant, but maybe you should check it out."

Dr. Maxwell had her lie back on the table. He probed the spot with his fingers. "It is not the implant," he said. "I am going to send you for a CAT scan as soon as possible."

From the CAT scan, the doctor found the cancer had metastasized in the liver. He did think there was a possibility that the lesion might be something other than cancer, so he scheduled an ultra sound before doing a biopsy. When the ultra sound confirmed the CAT scan report, Lois refused to have a biopsy. She did not think it necessary to subject her body to such an invasive procedure.

Lois now knew she had a form of cancer for which there was no cure and she made the decision to not take chemotherapy. She told her oncologist, Dr. Eric Raesky, "If I had a cancer that could be cured, there is no doubt I would take chemo."

"Lois," Dr. Raesky asked, "are you sure?"

"I have worked so long with Hospice, I am more comfortable working with death than working with chemo."

"You are a rarity," he said, shaking his head. "I have patients in their eighties and nineties with incurable diseases who take everything I can give them."

Lois's body was still producing hormones at the time of her first cancer, but the doctors had told her she would be a good candidate for hormone replacement therapy when she started going through menopause. The cancer had been so small, her doctors knew they had gotten it all.

About a year before her second diagnosis, Lois had started taking hormones. She felt this treatment did not cause the cancer, "but I was really fertilizing it," she said.

Lois did agree to try anti-hormonal therapy. This treatment blocked the hormones her body was producing. It pushed the cancer back twenty-five percent and held for two years. Lois felt this allowed her body to maintain its health without involving her immune system.

Then the cancer started growing again. The doctor said that if she did not take the chemo he suggested, she would be dead in two or three months.

"Will there be side affects?" she asked.

"This is a new treatment," she was told, "and so far the side affects have been minimal."

Lois was hesitant. "If you start chemo, you will have to have a CAT scan and a chest X-ray," the doctor said.

Lois decided she would take the tests even if she was undecided about taking chemotherapy. The nurse set up the appointment.

When Lois went into the waiting room, she spoke to the two African-American women seated there. Then she was called to the back by a beautiful young technician, who was also African-American.

"I am so nervous," Lois said, and then she told the young woman her anxiety about taking chemotherapy. "I don't know if I am supposed to have it or not. I have prayed about this, but I have not had an answer."

"I am a minister," the girl said, and she got down on her knees with Lois and prayed for her.

Lois went back into the waiting room and began to tell the two women what had happened. The older of the two walked over and took her hand. "I am a missionary, and I will pray for you, too."

Lois sat there, thinking, I don't have to be hit over the head. This is what I am supposed to be doing. God is putting a blessing on me at every turn.

She started chemotherapy knowing she had done the right thing. The chemo gave her a year before it stopped working. Again, she refused more.

"You could be dead within a month," the doctor said.

When Lois began to have pain and nausea, she called the doctor.

The doctor gave her more chemo with good results. Some of the tumors were smaller, but most importantly, there were no side effects.

Lois finished up her practice, but continued speaking to groups on the subject "Living with Dying."

One day Lois and Wayne were leaving Radnor Lake when a woman stopped them. Wayne got out of the truck to talk with her.

"I just saw a deer with a broken leg," she began. "Poor thing, how will she be able to get enough to eat? She needs to be put down."

"That doe has been around here for a long time, and we watch out for her. So far it hasn't been necessary to destroy her," Wayne said.

"The last time I saw her she was with her new baby and a large buck was standing close by," Lois said to Wayne as he got back in the truck. "She may have a broken leg, but everything else seems to be operating pretty well.

"What a wonderful story this is," she said. "I will use this when I speak, for that doe is a wonderful example of living with a challenge.

"I forget how other people look at things," she said, and was quiet until they got home. As they went into the house, Lois said, "I was just thinking about people I have known with challenges. I had a friend whose uncle took us water skiing. He had lost a leg, but he skied, drove the boat, and did what everybody else did.

"In the seventh grade I had a Sunday school teacher who had had polio. She wore a brace and was a wonderful inspiration for me. There was a boy in a wheelchair. He must have had muscular dystrophy, but he always smiled and spoke to everyone.

"These were people who have been in my life intimately. They influenced the way I looked at the world, for I saw them living fulfilled lives and I saw them happy.

"I learned years ago never to look with pity on people who have challenges," she said, and went into the kitchen to start supper. "I have tried to educate others by asking them if they really needed to spend their sympathy that way." She was peeling potatoes and she pointed the knife at Wayne. "I don't think pity helps anyone."

"I agree," Wayne said and smiled. "I have heard you tell people in wheel chairs so many times that they ought to tie bells and ribbons on them. You celebrate everything."

"They have more difficult stuff going on than I do," she said. "Of course they wish they had what others have, but most would not want another life because they have adjusted." Lois knew it was just a matter of perceptions, and she often admonished people to not talk to those in wheel chairs as if they were retarded and to speak to them, not the person pushing them.

"I have learned so much from you," Wayne said.

Lois smiled and put down the knife to give him a hug.

"I have done so many things in my adult life," she said, "things I had always wanted to do but didn't have the opportunity when I was a child."

"Such as?" Wayne asked.

"Well, in Huntsville I took ballet because I didn't get to take dancing when I was young." She laughed, "When the teacher wanted me to be an angel in a pink tutu, I said 'Sorry, I don't do tutus,' and I didn't participate in her revue."

Wayne could not help but smile at the thought of Lois in a pink tutu.

"I also learned to ride a bike, and I got to go horseback riding."

As they were eating, Lois frowned and said, "I have been asking myself what is it that I have always wanted to do. I know I need to do it soon or I may never get the chance."

"And what is that?" Wayne asked.

"There's more than one thing," Lois said as she laughed. "The most exciting thing I can think of is rafting down the Colorado River. And I have always wanted to take a motorcycle ride."

"Well, let's just plan to do those very things," Wayne said.

11

Soon after this discussion with Wayne, Lois attended a workshop. There she reconnected with Sherry Lawler, a social worker she had met years before.

"How have you been?" Sherry asked.

"I feel really good, but I had a recurrence of my cancer and have had more surgery," Lois answered and went on to explain.

"What is happening with you, Sherry?"

"I am on my way to Hawaii," Sherry said, smiling broadly, "for a yoga retreat."

"I have been doing yoga for years," Lois said. "It is wonderful. I really envy you that trip."

"Well, what the heck—there is a space left. Want to come along?"

"I think so," Lois slowly answered and got all the information.

Lois had to take a different flight, but she arrived in Hilo and joined her friend at the Kalani Hanova Retreat in the Puna District. It was a gorgeous spot, with its black sand beach. Lois had not been so active and so busy since she was a child. She loved it.

For ten days she did yoga in the morning for two hours and in the afternoon for two more. She had never run for more than two miles, but now she and Sherry were running four miles each day. The vegetarian meals, which they ate outside in the beautiful weather, were delightful. After the last yoga session each day, they were free to play. One high point was sunning on the nude beach which had black sand, but the most important gift from this trip would be a new set of friends.

During the Hawaii trip Sherry and Lois connected with Martha Morgan and Margaret Johnson, and the four became fast friends. They immediately planned another trip, this time to Navarre Beach, Florida.

They had less than a week together, but they had a great time. A highlight of that trip was the water bug.

Sherry came into the kitchen and began to laugh. "Where did you get that fake bug?" she asked Lois. "It's too big to fool anyone."

Lois walked over to the table. "Oh," she said and began to laugh too. "That is real," and she reached to pick it up.

"Wait!" Sherry said. "Margaret," she called, "come and bring the camera." A picture of the uninvited guest was quickly taken.

At this first get-together, they decided to call themselves the "Girlfriends" and celebrate everyone's birthday.

It was October and Martha wanted to do something special for Lois's birthday. She talked with Sherry and Margaret and their gift was dinner on the "General Jackson," a paddlewheel dinner boat on the Cumberland River.

Whatever the means of celebration, it was always a surprise to the birthday girl. For Sherry they went to Roan Mountain, Tennessee, making reservations six months in advance.

Lois believed in celebrations, and this birthday was a joyful occasion. She told Sherry, "This should just be the beginning. You know I celebrate my birthday all month. All year might be better," she added and laughed.

"I really don't like the getting older part," someone said.

"I don't worry about that," Lois spoke up. "I think of birthdays as the time God brought me into the world, and I feel that my very being is something to celebrate. There are so many rough spots and so much sadness in life," she said, "we need to build in these happy times to even it out."

For one birthday celebration the "Girlfriends" went for glamour shots. Lois had lost half her hair and was not wearing much makeup. "I am just glad to be alive," she said. But when she saw the pictures, "Wow!" she exclaimed. "I look drop-dead gorgeous." She chose this picture for the thank-you cards Wayne would send after her death.

When Lois began to have physical problems from the cancer, Wayne went with the "Girlfriends" whenever they went out of town. After going to Roan Mountain on a weekend trip, Margaret wrote, "Wayne is one of the best 'Girlfriends' we have ever had."

On her next birthday, Lois was not feeling well. She knew she would be going to Sherry's house, but she did not know what to expect.

She was greeted at the door with "Come in and take off your clothes." She was given a long white robe with a big "L" on the left shoulder—for Lois, not Laverne. There was a lounge chair in the middle of the den. They put Lois in the comfortable chair, lit candles, and proceeded to pamper her to the nth degree. There was a massage, then a facial, a manicure, a pedicure, and all the while someone was fanning her. Two other members of the Hawaiian trip—Patti Zimmerman and Kathy Felts—were included in the "Pamper Party."

The party ended with grilled lobster and a birthday cake, with black sand and nude bathers, reminiscent of what they had seen in Hawaii.

"Remember that beach?" Martha asked as Lois blew out the single candle.

"Do I!" Margaret said.

"I wanted to help that dying man," Lois said, and they all laughed.

They had been curious about the nude beach and gone to check it out when they saw a man being dragged from the water. They thought he was dead. She and Margaret ran over to get the people pulling the man to lay him down on the sand. To die peacefully, Lois thought.

Lois put her hand on his leg. She knew the power of touch and wanted to calm him and make the end as peaceful as possible for this man she did not know.

The man sputtered, spat out sand, and slowly began to recover. Later they found out he had been smoking pot before he had gone into the water. Martha, who was a swimming teacher and a strong swimmer herself, said, "I swam in this ocean once, but I won't again because of the strong undertows." She frowned, "But to go into the Pacific Ocean impaired by drink or drugs is really taking your life in your hands."

That night someone asked Lois, "Will you smoke pot now that you have this cancer that could kill you?"

She laughed, "I have smoked pot, and I had what I call 'another world' experience." She became very serious, "I think that happens to others, too, but some won't admit it. But anyway, why would I want to be in another world when I have so little time left in this one? I'm not willing to be in an artificial reality when this one is so dear," she emphasized.

As they talked about the man they thought had drowned, Lois, ever the therapist, said, "If he doesn't know the rules by now, he would benefit from a Twelve-Step Program."

"I thought from his color he was already gone," said Margaret. At the time they were shaken by the experience, but now they could laugh about it.

The reminder of Hawaii gave Lois the idea for a quit-smoking celebration. Patti had stopped smoking during that time. Lois had smoked and knew how hard it was to quit. She wanted to do something to honor her friend's accomplishment. Lois gave God credit for the idea and knew it would come to pass.

The next morning, she was running at Radnor Lake. She rounded a corner and spoke to a man she had not seen there before. She realized that he had had a tracheotomy and stopped to tell him about her plan. She found out he was a neighbor of hers and had stopped smoking two years before cancer was discovered. Now he did public speaking on the subject of cancer and smoking. Bill said, "Of course I want to be a part of that celebration."

Lois contacted the American Lung Association and spoke to Shelia Marczak.

"That sounds interesting," Shelia said. They met and called in people from other groups and the "X-Smokers Celebration" was born.

"This will be a good experience for people who still smoke and would like to quit. They will meet people just like themselves who did quit and found their lives were better because of it," Lois said. Other members of the group agreed.

"We will need something entertaining," one said.

Lois thought about Aashid Himmons. "I know this man who has a band called 'African Dreamland.' They play blue reggae and have been a hit around Nashville for years. But the reason he would be perfect for this occasion is the fact that he had to stop smoking." Lois called and Aashid did agree to join in the celebration.

The date was set: September 14, 2000. There was a clown, and Lois found a bagpiper. "I can't think of a better example to show why one shouldn't smoke," Lois said. She asked her friend, Marian Dunn, to speak on what tobacco meant to the American Indian. Hills' grocery chain provided helium-filled balloons. Although they had chosen a week night, there were as many as 200 people present at one time.

A group in Chattanooga picked up on the idea, set a date, and asked Lois to attend. At the time of their celebration her health made it impossible for her to go, but she was thrilled that people were willing to see the power in such a celebration.

The "Girlfriends" were Lois's support group. She always made a point of seeking out people who thought as she did. "You are as healthy or unhealthy as the friends around you," she often said. As the birthday celebrations continued, they never fussed. When they got together, it was a time of love, peace, and joy.

12

Lois and Wayne finalized their plans for a rafting trip down the Colorado River. Lois had thought it would sap more of her energy than it did, but she made the trip without any adverse affects. She told Wayne, "This was more like a spiritual journey, and I never felt closer to God. It is so hard to put into words, but it was like being in no time, and all time, and before time. I felt I was in the womb of the earth."

Wayne understood perfectly.

On her fifty-eighth birthday, Wayne presented her with a beautifully-wrapped box, containing a picture of a motorcycle helmet. He had asked Jeff, his boss at Radnor Lake, about a motorcycle trip for Lois.

"If she goes at all," Jeff said, "It must be down the Blue Ridge Mountains."

Wayne knew Jeff to be an experienced and knowledgeable rider. With Wayne following in a van, Jeff, with Lois on the back of his motorcycle, headed down the Blue Ridge Mountains in North Carolina.

Lois was scared to death. She said to herself, I can either hold on for dear life and hate every minute of this ride, or I can relax, sit back and look at the beautiful scenery. She chose the latter and enjoyed a wonderful five-hour ride. Then they celebrated her birthday even more by soaring in a glider over this beautiful area.

Lois also had the desire to go to Africa. She knew she would have gone sometime, but her diagnosis made it sooner. One night she awoke from a sound sleep. "Wayne," she called loudly and sat up.

He jumped. "Are you all right?" he asked.

"Oh, yes," she answered, "I just wanted to tell you, we have to go to Africa."

"Okay," he said calmly. "When?"

"Soon as we can," she said and lay back down.

Later, Lois asked Wayne why he so readily agreed and answered as he did. He smiled at her and said, "I am so used to doing whatever you suggest." Then he took her hand and looked into her eyes, "But when it is inspired, just coming out of nowhere, it becomes a spiritual experience."

"You are right," she said. "God-given."

Lois began searching for anything she could find on Africa. She found out about a travel agency named Park East, called them and got their literature. "We want to see the animals," she said, and their trip was narrowed down to Kenya and Tanzania. Lois had the feeling she was going home and later found out this was not unusual for many people felt that way about Africa: white and black. She remembered reading that through DNA, it was proven that we were descendants from "Lucy," an African woman of prehistoric time.

Lois gained more insight from the trip. Most members of the tour kept comparing Africa with the United States and felt very sorry for the people. Lois did see women getting water from dirty streams and saw poverty of material things, but she saw even more. She saw a people close in spirit. The Africans sat together. There were families eating together, talking, and showing a great deal of love for one another. She knew that in the United States families did not eat together and did not talk to each other any longer. Back home there was often a distance between parents and children, as well as husbands and wives.

"Who is the real third world country?' she asked Wayne as they were waiting at a railroad station. They had just observed an African mother calm her crying baby by rubbing his face. She held the baby in her arms and, not just lightly, but firmly rubbed her hands over his forehead, down his cheeks, and across his head as she poured out her love for him.

"Who is really in poverty?" Wayne asked.

Lois was looking for a spiritual experience since she felt she had been told by God to go Africa, but what happened was a stronger realization of what she already knew. When they were out in the bush, her temperature went up and her energy level went down. I am going to die in Africa, she thought. Lois had known this could happen before they even left on their trip, but being in Africa and realizing she might not get home was quite different.

Wayne went to dinner, which was served out in the bush on tables covered in white cloths and loaded with silver and china. Lois lay in bed, praying. "God, what am I supposed to know?" she asked. "This feels pretty heavy, and I am so far from home." God gave her to understand that she was not away from home because He was there. She was in God's hands, whether she died in Africa or Nashville. She was no longer scared.

Later, when she recounted this story, someone would invariably ask, "Did you get healed? Did the temperature go down?"

"No," she would say. "I still felt like crap, but woke up with peace of mind."

Her spirit was healed. Most people think healing is of a physical nature, but Lois always maintained that through the cancer she was healed spiritually and mentally.

Lois received many gifts from this trip. One was their guide. The first night she met Peter, she was not mingling at the introductory cocktail party, but was sitting by herself, conserving her energy. He came over to question why she was alone. She told him her story. He asked, "Do you believe in God?" When she answered, "Yes," he said, "Then everything is all right, isn't it?"

Lois laughed and agreed. Peter became her watch person. They had another guide in Tanzania, but when they left the tour and flew back to Nairobi, Peter met their plane to help them through Customs.

Lois and Wayne left Africa with mixed feelings. Both felt the uniqueness of being a minority in a country of dark skin. "Quite an experience," Lois said, "but quite different from being at TSU."

The parks were enormous compared with those in the United States. "Seeing these beautiful animals in what appeared to be complete freedom was the highlight for me," Wayne told Lois. "Elephants without physical boundaries is like nothing I have ever seen before."

"Just seeing large and small animals in their natural habitat is divine," Lois said. "And seeing the elephants marching toward their own food, not food just put out for them, is amazing."

What they disliked was the unnecessary expense brought about by staying in four-star hotels that had been built for the very rich. "I am not used to plush, and don't live that way at home," Lois said, "or travel that way in the United States."

"We just need food and a place to be comfortable," Wayne agreed. "Not multi-course meals served out in the bush on china with real silver."

They were in a luxurious hotel, and fifteen miles down the road there were stands selling juice and old clothing that was used and reused because the country was so poor. "Seeing the level of their economy and how much we spent that could have been used to make life easier for the people here was difficult for me," Lois said, "but this has been a wonderful trip."

After her mother's death, Lois was angry and had completely turned away from God for a short time, but her faith had returned and was strongly in place before her first diagnosis. She was grateful that she had not had to struggle with that issue. To Lois, the gift in the cancer was realizing how precious life is, and this allowed her to open her heart to everything around her. After this trip to Africa, Lois knew God was with her all the time, but in a different way.

13

When Lois's health no longer permitted her to work in her private practice or do the extensive volunteer work she loved so much, she still spoke on "Living with Dying" to various professional groups. She felt she had learned so much about living with this incurable disease that she could help others. But how? She knew Gilda's Club was a wonderful emotional support community for people with cancer, so she contacted the program director, Felice Apolinsky.

"The work that I do is so important to me," Lois said. "It is so spiritual and so vital. It makes a tremendous difference when I am able to help people grow while living with dying. Felice, I have been speaking on this subject for the past year or more, and I was thinking there might be people who are members of Gilda's Club who could make use of what I have learned through my own diagnosis."

Felice was very interested.

"I have never heard of a group like this," Lois said, "and feel most professionals would say nobody would come." Felice laughed as Lois continued. "I want to open a door that anyone else would keep closed and bring out into the open what other people won't talk about. When I say I am dying, most people change the subject. My purpose will be to help people learn some things that have been beneficial to me."

Felice said, "I think it will be wonderful having a group where participants can talk about the fears associated with dying from an incurable disease."

"It has been my experience that people just want to prop me up and say, 'You'll be all right; don't worry,'" Lois said. "I want to empower this group to talk to their friends and say, 'Don't cut me off, I may not be healing.'"

The group was listed in the October 2000 calendar at Gilda's Club as "Living with Dying," a support group for people living with cancer who have been given a prognosis of limited time. They would meet for an hour and a half each Wednesday for a period of four weeks, and then Lois would begin another four-week session.

Lois felt that no group was random, and she saw God's hand on each of the seven people seated in front of her. There were five survivors and two caregivers.

Lois was seated in her favorite cross-legged position on a love seat with a glass of water in her hand. "Most of you know that chemotherapy, or the cancer itself makes your mouth dry, so you will seldom see me without my water." She laughed and took a sip as she introduced herself, then she said, "I would like each of you to give your name, and if you can, tell why you came to this group." Through this she hoped to find out what each had experienced, what they knew about themselves, and what they were feeling. "Sometimes you cannot explain why you came, and that is all right too," she said, "but you're here, and that's the important thing."

Walter spoke first. He came by himself. "I was first diagnosed with prostate cancer, which has now invaded my bones. I have had radiation and chemo both. The chemo is no longer working, but my doctor is talking to a doctor at Johns Hopkins about a new treatment."

Joyce and her dentist husband Sam had been married 35 years. "I have multiple myeloma," Joyce said. "I had a stem-cell replacement which put it in remission for two years, and I am taking chemo."

"If she begins to have pain, I am hoping the doctor will try radiation," Sam said. "It seems there has been a lot of success with radiation relieving pain."

Bob and Nancy had been married twenty-seven years. "I am retired. In January I thought I had pulled a muscle," Bob said, "but in May I found out that I have lung cancer. There is a tumor along my spine and a spot on my liver." Bob was on oxygen and it was obvious that he was in pain.

Amon was twenty-nine years old and diagnosed with a malignant brain tumor. A social worker from the rehab hospital where he was getting therapy had brought him. "I lost the use of my left arm about a year ago," he said. "I would yawn and that arm would raise, and I had nerves jumping on the left side of my face. The cancer was diagnosed when I went to the doctor because I couldn't hold anything in that hand and it was interfering with my work."

Betty had come alone. "I have three children," she said. "They are three, five, and eight. A year ago I had a mastectomy, but now there is a spot on my right lung."

Lois then asked each person what they expected from being there. One caregiver said, "I signed us up because I thought it would be about living with cancer."

Lois knew others probably felt the same way. "You thought there would be talk about living with dying but not talk about the actual dying process," Lois said. Heads nodded in agreement.

Lois looked around the room and smiled broadly. Her eyes twinkled. "Well, that is not exactly the case," she said. "We are not going to share poetry and then focus on living. We are going to talk about dying."

As the others talked about their diagnoses and their families, Lois realized that Walter did not feel comfortable. She sensed his nervousness and anxiety when he talked. She was not sure if this was from his diagnosis, being in the group, or whether he had a problem with the decision he was making. He discussed the new treatment by saying it "might work." Lois knew he did not mean a treatment that might buy more time, when he also used the words "can cure."

Lois had experience with people in denial. The mechanism of denial was so strong that if it was taken away there would have to be time to put the person back together again. That would not be possible in this group. Since Walter was manifesting something that told her he was not ready to deal with what the others were saying about their situations, she became very protective of him.

This was not the same as it was for Betty. This young mother only came to the first meeting. Betty was in her late thirties and had three young children. She had something that could not be cured and was looking at her children, knowing she was not going to see them grown. Lois knew mothers and fathers would do anything they could to stay alive one more day to see their children graduate from high school, then college, and be there when they got married and had children of their own. Betty was not in denial, but her reality was to scrape every bit of time she could manage. Lois knew Betty would not be able to accept that she was going to die until it actually happened. Later, when Lois explained this to the group, who were distressed not to see Betty any more, she said, "Betty may even feel guilty because she may not achieve seeing her children grown."

"How horrible," someone said, "to have guilt feelings over something you can do nothing about."

"That is why it is so important to send her our love and prayers," Lois said.

Lois knew it was way too soon for Amon to be facing death. He was such a beautiful young man. The brain tumor had left him with physical difficulties. His left foot would not work properly, and he did not have the use of his left arm. He did not have a personal caregiver, so he had to struggle with getting to doctors, getting to the grocery store, and cooking his own meals. Lois was quite concerned that she could not help in this area. She did know about some services in the community, but she did not know the requirements for getting their help. She would try to put Amon in touch with someone who could assist him.

Amon's sister Lisa had gone to Louisiana, where he was living, to bring him to the hospital where she worked as a nurse. A neurosurgeon told the family that the tumor could be debulked, but it would only give Amon three additional months, so he did not recommend the surgery.

Amon's mother lived in New York. He went home with her, and she found a surgeon who gave him a better prognosis. He had the surgery and began taking chemotherapy in pill form before returning to Nashville. Lisa had wanted Amon to live with her, but she had her own family and their apartment was small. The cancer made Amon extremely nervous, and as a result, he moved to a group home. This proved to be a very unsatisfactory arrangement. Some roommates took his food from the shared kitchen, and some were rowdy and disturbed his sleep. The home was not in the best neighborhood, and there were break-ins.

After he left the rehab hospital and could no longer have the social worker bring him, members of the group picked him up and brought him to the Wednesday meetings. "This is the highlight of my week," he said many times.

By making connections with each person's age and the developmental stages they had gone through, Lois was able to get a clear sense of how much each person knew about himself or herself. She was aware that Amon had not experienced as much of life as the others. After all, what had she known at his age? She knew he would have a harder time facing what she was going to be presenting.

Joyce began talking about her husband. "He is on the computer as soon as he gets home, running off pages and pages of information." She looked at Sam. "His need to know drives me crazy."

"Well, you can find out everything on the Internet," he said, "and there might be something new that hasn't reached here yet."

"I think the doctor would get that information as soon as you," his wife said, frowning.

Sam laughed.

As everyone talked, Lois had an opportunity to bring up things that related to what each was talking about. Bob talked about Billy, his stepson, who had died at age nineteen. Bob talked about the relationship they had had and how much he grieved for the young man. Lois did not know if he would talk more about Billy, but as the group went on, she hoped each would bring up a death near to them and talk about how that death could have been different. She would try to show

how they could have grieved more easily if their hearts had been more open to death, less like her experience with her mother's death. She was going to do everything she could to get that point across. Bob had given her a wonderful opportunity, so she made a note to ask him, at the fourth and last session of this group, what he had learned from Billy.

"It is easy for us to talk about physical matters, such as pain and medications," Lois said, "and you can talk to almost anyone about that. But you cannot talk to just anyone about the pain of losing someone or your fears about death." She looked around the room and began to laugh. "And we will talk about BMs," she said, "because no one feels comfortable about that subject, even with a nurse."

Lois used her skills to mold the group. If they tried to take the easy way out by talking only of physical matters, she would lead them back to what the group was about. With Walter, she knew she could not push and probe into his denial. He did come back for the second meeting, but he told Felice, "I don't need this group. I will be doing my new treatment in a couple of weeks."

Lois realized that Walter would not come to the group, even if he decided not to have the new procedure. But if he tried the treatment with poor results, he might be able to deal with his issues in a way he was not ready for now.

Less than two weeks later, Walter went to the hospital and, sadly for his family and many friends, died there.

Lois was pleased with the progress of this initial meeting. She knew the prognosis of those in the group who had cancer, and as they talked she learned just where they were with it. At this first meeting she was not only hearing about physical problems, but seeing how the group related to each other. She saw that Bob talked about his feelings and would be able to add to the group. She knew Amon had doubts about his memory and was worried about being on target or coming from left field. Joyce was all heart, but she knew Sam could get angry and would be her biggest challenge. This group had serious issues, but Lois knew that if they felt safe, they would talk about them and learn from each other.

All who came back for the second meeting knew what they would be dealing with. Had the majority not come back, Lois would have felt she had stepped too deeply into issues they were not ready to face. As each talked, she realized that Bob wanted to come back and talk about his fears. He was facing them and wanted to do something about them. Lois knew he had a sense of being in a family with people who understood.

Some of the members had attended other sessions at Gilda's Club, such as the Laughter and Self-Hypnosis Groups, with good results. But they left with the same issues that had brought them there in the first place. Lois's group allowed its members to get down to the basic facts of life and death, and they felt safe.

Bob's caretaker had spoken of her own issues from the time of their Newcomer's Meeting, which all members and volunteers were required to attend. "Poured my guts out," Nancy said as she spoke of the two children she had buried. When a beautiful baby girl had lived only six days, the father, her first husband, had said, "If it had been a boy, it might have bothered me."

"That was serious abuse," Lois said.

"I held back my pain and became unable to cry. I still can't cry," Nancy said.

"That is so painful," Lois said, "because tears are healing."

"Two years later," Nancy said, "my son was born with almost the same congenital heart problem, but when he died I had Bob to give me support. I never told anyone I had three children."

"But how healthy of you to talk about it," Lois said. "Unfinished business is making itself known. If grieving is not finished and five or ten years later you have to deal with this problem, people won't know what you are crying for," Lois pointed out. "So much therapy is done with grief issues." Lois looked around the room. "You can tell how much grief work you have done, or not done, with one death when you go to the next funeral and find yourself grieving for the last person who died."

She told Nancy, "These were very important losses. The death of a child is a tremendous loss. And here is this man who knew and loved Billy, and his death is coming up. You have enough grief on your shoulders."

"Is this why, when I heard Bob's diagnosis I felt like I was no longer strong, and was falling apart?"

"Exactly," said Lois.

Lois looked at Bob "Don't you feel the barriers breaking down between you each time you come to group?" she asked.

"Yes," he said. "This group has made a difference."

Lois looked at Sam and Joyce. Sam laughed, "It has been the same for us, too."

To make this a really strong group, Lois knew she had to be clear about where it was going. From the beginning she said, "Death is hidden, and we hurt because of it. My purpose is to bring death out into the open and share things that have been beneficial to me. You do not have to talk about anything you don't want to," she assured them. She knew Nancy felt safe and comfortable in the group. She will leave empowered, Lois thought. My work is good; God is good.

Amon felt his mother did not want to talk to him about dying. Lois asked how she had dealt with death in the past.

"She went into her bedroom and shut the door," he said, "but I do feel her sadness at my being sick. I am causing her a lot of pain."

Lois looked at Nancy and said, "If this were your son, what would you say to him?"

Nancy looked at the young man. "It is painful watching you be sick, but I wouldn't have missed knowing you for anything in the world." Tears formed in her eyes. "I love you," she said, "and am so sorry about what you are going through."

Amon laughed out loud. "I made Nancy cry," he said, and the other members laughed too.

"Good for you, Amon," Lois said. "Tears are healing."

Lois looked around the room. "Death is such a part of life, you cannot take responsibility for another person's grief," she said. "Time will help them get through the pain."

When Amon's mother was in town she came to Gilda's Club with him. The group made her feel welcome and hoped they gave her some comfort.

Lois talked to the group about her years with Hospice. "There was a family I visited," she said. "The man was dying and the doctor had called in Hospice. I was assigned to do the intake interview, so I called the house. I talked to the wife, and during our conversation I told her anyone could be there as long as it was all right with the patient." Lois smiled broadly, "I want you to know when I arrived there were so many children and grandchildren seated around the kitchen table that they had to find me a chair."

After the introductions, Lois asked the Hospice patient what he was most afraid of. He did not hesitate. "I am worried about how my wife is going to make it in the world without me."

"I try to be prepared, since I never know what the answer to that question will be," she told the group. "It could have been about unpaid bills, or not being able to take care of himself, a relationship that is in trouble, or about dying itself. But I always try to focus on whatever answer is given.

"This couple had been together many years. We talked about the love they had for each other and how hard it was going to be for her to lose him. I may have even asked if this love was worth the pain she was going to have, but I did ask him if he thought she was a pretty strong person. He said he thought so.

"I asked the children what part they saw themselves playing in their mother's life when their father would no longer be there to take care of her. After they talked about how they would check on her, cut the grass, take her to the store, and various other things, I asked the father if he could trust these children. 'In the past, when they said they would do something, did they follow through?' He assured me that they were trustworthy.

"So we faced his fear and worked out a solution."

Lois paused to take a sip of water. "Gilda's Club will set up a meeting with your family and friends to talk over concerns and ways each of them can help. There will be a facilitator who is knowledgeable and can steer everyone in the right direction. You may want to consider this," she told the group, thinking what a help this could be for Amon.

Lois spoke about living wills and a durable power of attorney, emphasizing how necessary they were to insure a person received the exact treatment they wanted. "There is a man in another state," she said, "who is in his fifties and has been brain dead for a number of years. His children have grown up during this time, and they have agreed to take him off the machine. But his mother has not agreed, so he remains on the machine. Doctors talk to family members, and if just one disagrees, they only listen to that one.

"I had an elderly neighbor, a Mrs. Jefferson," she continued. "She was in her nineties, lived alone, and had serious health problems. She didn't have children, but had one sister. Mrs. Jefferson moved into a nursing home. As her life played out, she was ready to die. She just didn't want to be around anymore. When she had a heart attack, I reached the nursing home just as they were putting her into the ambulance.

"'Please don't do anything,' I told them. Since there was no living will, they had to do everything they could, but I asked, 'Could you move slowly and not as quickly as you usually do?'

"Then I rushed over to the hospital and asked for the chaplain. I told him I had known this woman twenty years, loved her, and she was ready to go. He listened, got in touch with the sister, and the doctors only administered calming medication. I went with Mrs. Jefferson to the cardiac unit and cradled that sweet little head in my arms, humming hymns until she went to glory. If I had not been there, they would have plugged her into a machine and would not have extracted her for days or weeks.

"Another thing I didn't know about until I was talking to an organ donor group is that people are dying from lack of organs, and people are dying every day with perfectly healthy ones. Because we stand back from death, don't discuss it, and don't plan ahead, those organs get buried.

"And that reminds me of funerals," she continued. "If you have unlimited funds and want the most expensive funeral in the world, fine. But what often happens is people with limited funds see a funeral as the last way to show respect. They go in debt for years to pay for it. If they could have asked the person who died, they would have been told, 'Bury me like I lived—simply.'"

"I know someone who did that very thing," Sam said.

Lois shared more of what she had learned over the years. "Be prepared for hunger to be an issue," she said. "That is so hard on families to accept because that is part of our care-taking role—feeding and keeping up nourishment. We tend to think that if our loved one just eats, everything will be okay, but we are trying to feed someone who is in the dying process. We would be better off if we let them decide. Yes, they may get weaker if they don't eat, and they may have problems if they don't eat, but the dying do not need food. Food is for healthy people to get well. You don't need to withhold food, but offer small amounts so as not to overwhelm them. Try their favorite foods, but remember that taste buds change from the illness, meds, and chemo.

"I also praise any family for choosing Hospice care. Most people would choose to die at home. After my liver diagnosis, I bought a four-poster bed because home is where I want to be; and I want a pretty bed to die in." She took a sip of water and smiled. "Of course the bedroom was too feminine for Wayne, and I knew he wouldn't change it, so I took the posts down. We now have a ceiling fan, and I am enjoying my bed just as much."

"I am telling you this because it is a wonderful gift to die at home, but it is also a sacrifice. It is important that caregivers spell each other so no one is left to do all the work."

She looked at Nancy and Sam. "It is very important, when taking care of someone else, to keep connections with your own life. The more strings you can keep, like playing golf once a week or eating lunch with friends at least once a week, the easier it will be for you both now and later on. You can only take the best care of someone else if you are taking the best care of you. Taking care of yourself sometimes takes second place, but you can still tend to your sleep and nutritional needs.

"I want my family to grieve for me as much as they need to, but get back into life as soon as they can. We came up with a list of day trips and hobbies for Wayne, because when you are grieving you can't think of much else. Now he will be able to look at his list and say, 'I can do that.'

"I was a nurse and trained to be a caregiver. I feel most women know how to take care of others, but don't know how to redirect that to themselves. It is simple; you do the same thing for yourself that you do for other people.

"Ask yourself, 'What does another human being in my circumstances need?' Protect yourself. Work, but learn how to drop it and play. I know that there are just so many hours that I have, and I have to take care of me, so I must organize my work and leave it at the end of the day.

"I am telling you about Hospice," Lois continued, "so that you will know you can call them in any time you have stopped taking radiation or chemotherapy. When I refused to take chemo, I called in Hospice," Lois said "That way I got to know them and how they would take care of me with my meds and talking to the doctor, but as soon as I started the new chemo, I lost Hospice. I am just recommending that you get an assessment and see what they have to offer any time you are between treatments."

As she had said so many times before, Lois added, "What makes the difference is making an informed choice."

As Sam and Joyce talked more, Lois asked the group members if they had any advice for them.

Bob said to Joyce, "I really sympathize with you. I don't want to know so much about my disease."

Lois knew Sam had a need to know and felt in control getting that information, but it was not Joyce's need. Lois asked Joyce, "What do you do in the doctor's office? Do you close your ears?"

"My doctor and Sam talk while I'm taking chemo," she answered.

"I hope that is not hurting your feelings," Lois said to Joyce before turning to Sam. "So what you are doing is collecting the information, and that is your right, but do you demand that she read it? Do you try to get the doctor to read it?"

"Her oncologist has really been up-to-date on this information. I just chat on-line with others who have the same diagnosis and are doing the same treatment to see how they are reacting and if it is helping." He looked at his wife, "But I don't insist she read anything."

"It has gotten better since we have been coming here," Joyce said and laughed. "I guess he knows I would tell on him if he got too pushy."

"I love her and want her to get well," he said.

Lois saw tears form in Sam's eyes and wondered if he found something new, would he press his wife to use it or put the doctor to the test if she refused.

"If there is something to be found, not just for you," Lois said to Joyce, "but any of us," she said and looked around the room to include the whole group, "I think it is important to ask what are going to be the side affects and what are the benefits? These are questions people don't usually ask, but I know I would be willing to put up with the negatives of a treatment if there were very few or no side effects at all."

Lois reached for her water. "I don't go to the doctor planning to do battle with him, but I am the one who knows myself best. After a CAT scan and ultrasound showed the cancer was in my liver, I didn't feel that my body needed an invasive procedure, so I refused to have a biopsy. I have agreed to chemo twice, but there is nothing left except chemo with terrible side effects, so now the answer is no. Each one of us gets to make that choice, and each one of us gets to change our mind because we change from day to day. We may think we have it solid, and tomorrow something may hit us and we are not so ready to stop all treatment. I have focused on no treatment as an option in the group, because this is the only place you are going to hear it. Doctors and nurses routinely don't tell and won't bring up what each of us has the right to know about, because we wouldn't want what they are offering. I want each of you to make informed decisions. I am under the impression that ninety-nine percent of us make uninformed decisions to get treatments which do not cure, and we suffer because of them. A doctor is vested in buying more time and it is hard for him to give up fighting a cancer that cannot be cured. He may have heard of a new drug that is in development and wants to keep you alive until it is approved.

"This is a lesson for all of us," Lois said, "we are here to support each other." She knew from what had been said that Sam was a wonderful caregiver. He had been with Joyce through the stem-cell replacement, keeping her at home and doing most of the nursing himself.

Lois looked at Joyce, and then at Sam. "She has this disease for which there is no cure, and this is really a precious time for you. We all need time to love each other and work out our issues so there is resolution, so when the time comes she will be ready to die and you will be ready to let her go. Love is the most important thing we are sent on earth to learn."

At the fourth meeting, Bob barely had any strength left, but it was important for him to be with people who understood what he was dealing with. Lois knew Billy, his stepson, had been a very important part of his life. The way Bob expressed himself, she knew he had received the ultimate gift and saw the blessing in Billy's death. She had experienced this herself and could recognize it in another person; she called it the "awe" experience. When Bob spoke, Lois could see the "awe" was there. As she had planned at the first meeting, Lois asked Bob what Billy had taught him.

Bob said, "I saw him wear a Milwaukee brace because of curvature of the spine, have trouble breathing because of his heart condition, and yet it didn't get him down." Again he talked about his love for his stepson.

"You saw in this young man, who had such a short time, just how precious life is," Lois said and then asked, "Because of him, did you feel you should do more with your life?"

"I guess I did, even if I didn't realize it," Bob answered, with tears in his eyes. "Nancy and I became Lay Ministers in our church, taking communion to shut-ins and to nursing homes.

"There was one wonderful gentleman from our church in the nursing home who did not recognize us, but when Nancy read the Twenty-third Psalm and we said the Lord's Prayer, he always seemed to remember them.

"And we were with two beautiful friends when they died: Gwen and Phyllis. They were great gals and Gwen was like family."

Nancy smiled, "I wiped Gwen's bottom more than I did my mother's in the two years it took cancer to take her."

Lois laughed, "I told you we would talk about BMs."

"You're right, death is an 'awe' experience," Bob continued. "Gwen's death was sad for me, but when Phyllis passed, I felt a release. I knew I was no longer afraid to die."

This was to be the last meeting, as Lois and Felice had planned this group to be of short duration. Lois knew there would be information shared, but she had not realized the depth these members were willing to go to on the subject of dying. They now knew how healthy it was to talk about their issues and concerns, and they wanted to continue. Another facilitator was discussed, and the members agreed to meet together until one could be found. When the second four week session did not materialize, the original "Living with Dying" group became an ongoing part of Gilda's Club, with Lois still its leader.

Anne was the first newcomer to join the group. The members told their stories, and then Anne said, "I was a nurse, but I haven't been able to work in a year. I was diagnosed with breast cancer in 1998. After one year, the cancer had metastasized in my spine and was inoperable. Three months later, cancer was found in my right hip. I have two girls, ages twenty-three and twenty-four, two older sons, and three grandchildren. My daughter Jennifer has moved here, and I would like for her to come to some of the meetings." Anne reached for a Kleenex. "My mother died of this same thing when I was in my twenties, and I remember how it was for me."

Anne's daughter came to the meetings, but hated going back to work with her eyes red from crying. Still, she came as often as she could.

One week Jennifer came by herself. "I think Mother says more to my brothers than she does to me or my sister," she said.

"How does that make you feel?" Lois asked.

"Left out."

"Can you ask her to tell you just what is going on?" Lois asked.

"I guess so," Jennifer said, "but I am not sure what to say."

The situation was discussed by the group and the young girl left, saying she would talk to her mother soon.

The next time she came with her mother Jennifer said, "We talked, and I feel better." Anne smiled and reached over to pat her daughter's hand.

Lois knew how hard it was for children to accept a parent's terminal illness. Often they did not have the coping skills, but sometimes there were just too many questions that could not be answered.

At another meeting, Lois again told the group to do their living wills and get a durable power of attorney. "I know when the time comes and I cannot communicate and life does not have any meaning for me in this physical body, I will be ready to leave it; so I don't want anything done to keep it here. And plan your funeral if there are certain things you want or do not want."

Joyce spoke up, "I don't want anything done when I die. No funeral, no fuss."

"Now, Joyce," Sam said. "You know that's not possible, and what about me?"

"Nothing," she repeated. "I don't want money wasted on a big show."

"It could be simple," he said.

"No," she said. "I know you and your idea of simple. You'll want to have a show for your professional friends." They began to argue.

Nancy finally interrupted. "Hey, just remember when she's gone, you can do whatever you want. She will never know."

Everyone laughed. "That's right," Lois said.

"I have planned Bob's funeral, and I will probably read," Nancy said.

When Bob said, "I knew you would," he set in motion the memorial service where his wife gave the eulogy when he died in January 2001.

Nancy knew she would want to set up a table depicting areas of Bob's life at his memorial service, and she began to go through their pictures. She made an album and gave it to him at Christmas as a love letter. He was so pleased; he looked at it often. After Bob died, his wife continued to come to the group. Often she brought Amon. At one meeting when he wasn't there, Nancy said, "I would like to take him home with me."

Lois said, "That wouldn't be healthy." The other members agreed.

"When you have heavy grieving to do," Lois said, "and take on a challenge like that, it would keep you from doing your grief work at the appropriate time." She smiled, "Amon is in your life so you can say the things you couldn't say to Billy."

"He called me his pseudo-mom," Nancy said, tears in her eyes.

"It was real healing for you, and a way to honor Billy. This is profound stuff," she said, smiling broadly.

At the next meeting two newcomers, Howard and Annemarie, joined the group. The survivor listened as Lois briefly told her story. "I have had breast cancer that came back after nine years and metastasized in my liver. My prognosis is not good." She smiled as she added with much enthusiasm, "I am enjoying the life I have left to its absolute fullest."

The others introduced themselves, and then the newcomers talked about their situation. Howard began. "I was diagnosed with prostate cancer seven years ago. Then three years ago I went into kidney failure from new tumors." As he talked, the group learned that he was a professor and taught a course on American Indian religion, as well as counseled graduate students.

His wife, Annemarie, taught at another college. "I took a leave of absence for this semester," she said, "to be with Howard."

"I regret that it is necessary for her to go back," Howard said. "The fact that she will need her job to survive after I am no longer here is one of my greatest concerns," he said, smiling at his wife.

"Although I could retire," he went on, "I feel more alive when I am teaching."

"Keep teaching as long as you can," said Sam.

"You must have meaningful relationships with your students," said Nancy.

"When Howard opened up about his illness to his students, he received so many affirmations of love and appreciation," said Annemarie.

"Yes, I did," Howard said emphatically.

"The people I worked with had a garage sale for me, and I really appreciated that," Anne said. "There was a book for everyone to write in. A doctor wrote how my illness had opened up his mind. When he saw how everyone went out of their way to help, he began to see a depth to people he had not seen before."

"Be open; give back the gift by letting others help," Lois said. "We are teaching people how to deal with someone who is sick and dying." Lois laughed as her eyes flashed. "You can even teach nurses and doctors."

Lois asked Annemarie about her role as caregiver, then said, "You feel you will have all the time in the world to rest when you are alone, but you need to take gentle care of you now."

Nancy said, "You have all the pain you can stand watching someone you love suffer, seeing them die, and missing them. But being in this group, talking to Bob about dying while he *was* dying, was a first for me. It made his passing easier, for I was able to say what I needed before it was too late."

Later, Lois asked Howard how he felt about the group.

"This has been good," he said. "I think this is where we need to be, and we will definitely be back." Annemarie nodded in agreement.

As Lois hugged him, Howard said, "You are so enthusiastic about life, in spite of your diagnosis; I want to know how to get there."

Lois really laughed at this. "I will try to show you," she said.

Lois began the next meeting by saying, "Another thing I like to ask about is where we are spiritually. I don't mean what religion a person is, for I could be talking to a Muslim or Buddhist family. Talking about God might offend, but talking about a spiritual connection brings it home to everyone. As I talked with the Hospice family I was telling you about, the patient said he was all right with his Maker, and I believed him. I will believe a person's answer to this, especially if the body language backs them up."

The group members began to talk about their various church affiliations and what they meant to them.

"Right now I do not go to church," Lois said. "I feel that people are my church; Radnor Lake is my church; this group is my church. But I believe the reason I am not afraid of death is my spiritual connection. Once I was talking to a group and a woman asked, 'Don't you think that being a Christian makes the difference?' Well, I didn't want to be ugly, but I have seen a number of Christians die who were pretty afraid. I think many die quietly and in peace with everything all right with their souls. I cannot speak for atheists, but I have seen them die. I had a really good friend who was caring and nurturing. He had the same ethics of someone with deep faith, and he had tremendous respect for other people. He was an atheist, and he died peacefully. I think it is the connection a person has with the world and perhaps the Creator that makes the difference.

"My attitude comes from the experiences I have had with dying people. It feels right to me to not fight the cancer. It's a matter of acceptance, but I do have this faith thing. I will focus on completing the work God has planned for me to do. When it is finished, God will take me home.

"It is not what you have been taught, but what you yourself have incorporated. Certainly, Christians do die secure in their faith. When I die, I will leave a world with all its problems and its junk," she smiled and added, "but it is still a wonderful world, in spite of all that. When I die I think I will go directly to God, to the light, to all knowing, to peace, to rest." She laughed. "There is nothing scary about that to me."

Lois: "I truly believe that many of the religions all over the world have the same basic beliefs and that it is arrogant of one to think they have the only answers and the rest have no validity. God made us all, and I believe presents Himself or Herself in different ways to different people. The important fact is to live up to the beliefs of your religion. It seems to me when we call ourselves religious and are so condemning of our fellow man, thinking what we believe is what everyone should believe, we have completely missed the point. So many people have been badly hurt by organized religions—such as my gay and lesbian friends—and much harm has been done by men using the Bible to keep women down. What really matters is loving each other and recognizing the

Divine Creator, the Great Spirit of the American Indian, the Buddha, or Christ.

"I was most offended when I was in the hospital once. People from the Baptist Nursing School wrote me notes, asking if I believed in Jesus Christ as my Savior, saying they wanted me to be saved so I could be with them in heaven. I wanted to write back, but then I talked to a Jewish friend. I thought he could help me, since they have had more trials and tribulations about not being Christian. He made me understand this was a mandate of their church, and anything I could say would not change a thing.

"I feel doubting is part of being human, and that is when your faith comes in. If I have doubts, I feel I have a choice. Do I follow that dark side, or do I follow the trust that I have had for so many days, so many hours, and so many years? Then I put myself in God's hands and let the angels watch over me.

Lois also taught the group about closure. "Tell your loved ones good-bye and tell them what they have meant to you and what they have taught you.

"I am not dying, thinking of things I haven't done," she said. "I just want to be with my son longer. I want to be with my husband longer. There is not a time I would say, 'I have had enough of you all, time to go to Heaven.' At the same time, when my body is racked enough with this disease and when there is not much of me left, it will be an easier good-bye.

"I have made it a point to call and thank people who have helped me along the way. I was able to thank the Crutchers—he was a photographer in Gallatin. He and his wife helped me feel better about myself in high school."

"What about someone you hate?" Sam asked.

Lois thought about that question. "I have tried very hard not to hate, because hating works against me," she said, "but I am human enough to not like some people."

Lois thought about a man she had worked with a few years before. He was conducting a panel on mental health and Lois was on the panel as she had been many times before. Lois had gone down to greet people, be sure they had the handouts, and guide them to the front seats. He had called her back to the stage. "You don't need to be down there in the audience," he said, and proceeded to criticize her behavior, her dress, and her demeanor. A friend who was also on the panel said to Lois, "I wonder what that was all about? It was uncalled for."

"If he had said something at one of our follow-up meetings I would have understood and acted differently," Lois said. "This was a surprise to me."

She immediately thought about needing closure with this man. Thank you, Sam, she said to herself, I knew I would learn from you.

Lois called the man and later told the group, "It worked beautifully. It was a wonderful healing. I wanted to let him know I felt attacked at the time and how it hurt our relationship. I put it in a positive frame, and it was wonderful to hear what he said back. He took full responsibility, apologized profusely, and asked what he could do to make it right." She laughed. "He did say he didn't remember the incident, but I felt a burden had been lifted from my shoulders that I didn't know was there. We had been very close, so I must have grieved over the years. It was so interesting, I wanted to share that feeling."

She laughed. "Of course it could have backfired and hit me in the face, but I was prepared for that too."

At another meeting Lois again talked about hospitals. "I will tell you why I think Hospice is so important in the dying process itself. Hospitals are geared to getting you well; they are not a place to go to die. They handle you differently, and they are a wonderful place to be if you can be cured of what ails you, but if you cannot be cured they generally don't give you the medications you need. They don't want us to get addicted," she said and laughed. "That is not a big concern of mine. If I get addicted, they can put my butt in treatment."

Lois looked around the room. "I feel comfortable here, don't you? This reminds me to tell you about going to the hospital, because in spite of what I have said, there may be a time when it is exactly where you need to be. Most people are not comfortable in a hospital. I am, because of my nursing background. I like the sounds and smells of a hospital, and I like to see uniforms. But when I go for a stay, I never go without a portable radio, relaxation tapes, nature tapes, and soothing music. When nurses are on a schedule and need to get things done on time, most people catch the energy and jump out of their skins. Actually, they have nothing to do with what is going on, since they are the patient and are in bed.

"I take pictures of people I love, pictures of dolphins, or post cards. I take small things that don't break, such as stones that are for healing and giving energy. With something to read—maybe a spiritual book that connects me with my Creator—I have my nest. I have a nest at home, and I make one in the hospital. Sometimes I have a minister come in and bless the space. Always before surgery I try to have a massage and a yoga session. That is my way of getting good oxygen into my body and relaxing it to make the surgery go well and to aid in the healing process.

"As a nurse, I knew I would only have two years to live when my liver became involved, although I have made it past three years now. This is not the same as cancer of the liver, which can be cured; metastasized to the liver is a different matter. Although I am fifty-eight, I had always thought I would live to be ninety or a hundred, so I do think I am dying prematurely." She then told the group about her Aunt Ethel, who was ninety-four her last birthday. "I have her genes and thought I would easily live as long a life as she has.

"She still lives alone, but is now legally blind from macular degeneration. This lady had lost a two-year old daughter, and she still talks about that beautiful child. Then her son had a brain tumor when he was in his thirties. She was working, but she went to the hospital and stayed every night. She was devastated when he died.

"Months later, she was in bed and having trouble sleeping. She opened her eyes and what light there was formed a cross on the wall. She got the word that God loved us enough to give up his Son, and if God could do that, she was given to understand that she could give up her son, be at peace, and rest in her faith. From that time on she loved her son and missed him, but she gave up her grief.

"When her eyes failed she sold her car and rejoiced that she did not have to buy insurance, gas, or do any more maintenance on an automobile. She realized she could get a cab whenever she needed to go and did not feel cut off from the world.

"Aunt Ethel came for a visit and went to a sight center where a blind person on the staff helped her to label clothes by dots so her colors matched, and they gave her a form that fit on her checkbook so she knew where to write and sign her name. She gave up her dignity and used a wheelchair in order to travel. It was this strength thing that made me think I could do as well." Lois laughed as she said, "And this woman can still bend over and touch her toes without snapping and cracking.

"Aunt Ethel has a granddaughter with Downs Syndrome. She is enormously proud of her, as we all are, because this girl has a job, lives on her own, and participates in the Special Olympics, winning many, many ribbons.

"This is a group of people I feel good about. When I was growing up, and I bet it was true of some of you," she said, looking around the room, "those children were carefully hidden away. Now you see them everywhere. These are the children who never get angry and are never demanding. They are the children who teach us how to love. Look at the gift we denied ourselves all those years because they were not good enough for us and had to be closeted!

"There is a woman who works at one of the fast food places who has Downs Syndrome. She is bright, willing to work, and enthusiastic. Wayne and I eat there often and find her a joy to be around."

Lois reached for her water. "So I will be dying before I am sixty," she said. "We don't have a choice about what happens to us, but we do have a choice in how we respond to it. I can see myself as 'poor Lois' who cannot run anymore, who is not going to see her son reach forty, and will not live a long full life with her husband. I can get really angry that this is not mine to do. But if I am involved with negatives, I miss out on what I do have, and then I can't appreciate the beautiful flowers the 'Girlfriends' send me, or enjoy my yard with all the trees and birds and the deer that come through, or enjoy my friends and family. There are people who put everything off until tomorrow or are waiting until they retire. I find that no matter what the age, people who open themselves to the experience of living are much more likely to release to death and make some sense out of whatever life they have had."

When her chemo stopped working, Lois did ask the group to accept her choice for a co-facilitator. "I have known Karen Wheeler for a long time, and she is like my sister. I think she will be just the one to help when I can no longer be a part of this group." The members accepted Karen readily.

When Lois made the decision to no longer come to Gilda's Club, some members were angry. "We push ourselves to come," one said. "I'm tired, too," said another.

Lois stopped going to the group in May, 2001. She had been so energetic, she found it hard to adjust to her loss of energy. More than ever, she carefully chose her activities in order to conserve her strength. The group was important to her, and she knew it should continue, but it would have to go on without her.

Amon's chemo had stopped working. His doctors tried laser surgery and then strong doses of Thalidomide, but this did not help. When his doctors called in Hospice, Lois encouraged Amon to consider moving to the Hospice Residence. Nancy took him to visit the facility. As he was leaving, he called Lois and said if he could get in, he thought he would move there, but then he said, "It means I'm going to die."

What did he think he was going to do in that other place? Lois wondered. Amon must be thinking he might as well give up. "You won't have to worry about groceries, cooking, and calling doctors. That will all be done for you," Lois said. "I think you will get such good care that you will have more strength to do other things."

When Amon did move into the residence Lois said, "We need to have a 'love-in.'" Wayne brought Lois, who was now in a wheel chair, and other members of the group came with balloons. There were hugs and much laughter, and Lois and Amon argued about who would get to Heaven first. Mike Rose from WTVF, NewsChannel 5 Network, was there.

The next month a new member joined the group. Jack came by himself. "I was diagnosed with pancreatic cancer and given three months to live. I don't know what to do," he said.

"Do you have any family?" someone asked.

"I have a daughter," Jack answered.

"How is she accepting your diagnosis?" Karen asked.

"She says she is sorry, kisses me, and then tells me, 'Remember I want your car,'" Jack said.

Tears formed as he talked. Joyce handed him a Kleenex. "Don't stop crying," she said, "It's good for you."

"My friends don't believe me, and I can't talk to them," Jack said.

"You can talk to us," Sam said, making Jack feel welcome.

Jack talked about his life and how this had hit him. "It is so sudden," he said.

As they talked, Nancy said, "I know this sounds cruel, but what your daughter said is something you should consider."

"Yes," Karen said, "You do need to get a will and plan what you want done. Do you have a living will?"

When Jack said, "No," she explained why he should consider having one drawn up.

"Get the paperwork behind you so you can concentrate on living," Sam said.

"This is the only place I have to talk about my cancer," Jack said. "I am so thankful for this group and for Gilda's Club."

When Karen called Lois and told her about Jack, Lois said, "I feel like I got a pat on the back from God."

As the group continued, Karen asked Felice to be co-facilitator.

14

Lois had spoken to many groups about "Living with Dying." Her last talk was to a group of nurses in Gallatin, Tennessee, at the hospital where she had started her career. Mike from WTVF, NewsChannel 5 Network, was there to film the session.

Lois was introduced by the Supervisor of Nursing as a woman who had a Ph.D. in living. "When Lois is given a mountain, she climbs to the top to see the view." Everyone laughed when the Supervisor added, "And sometimes she stops to beautify that mountain top."

Lois began by passing around her Love Book. For an hour she talked about what she had learned. She told of Gilda's Club. "God cupped His hand around my ear," she said. "I am so thankful to Him for allowing the 'Living with Dying' group to happen. It was extremely important to me.

"The real tragedy is to have someone die when there are unresolved issues," she said. "That is the advantage of knowing I am dying. I don't think my son and I have unfinished business, so he will only have to deal with grief. The more Wayne and I sort out, we won't have unfinished business either.

"From my profession, I have learned that death is a normal way of life. That is how I got to *There*. I have always been able to recognize important moments."

When she finished, she got a standing ovation. "That is a first," she said and smiled broadly.

It wasn't long before Lois began what she called "The Sweetness of Leaving."

She had as many visitors as her failing energy allowed. A friend she had not seen in a year called, and they had a wonderful visit. The woman said, "I had thought this would be so hard, but I am glad I came. A lot of your friends are afraid to come; they can't stand to see you in this condition."

"Tell them they are missing out," Lois said. "It is sad that everybody thinks this dying thing is ugly." She smiled. "I am not as pretty as I was because I have lost weight." She paused. "Most people think of weddings or having babies as the happy part of life, but funerals and people dying is magic. This is truly a magical time. We are in touch with the Divine if we are ever going to be, and we are willing to share the experience."

Lois felt that when her friend left she was able to deal with death in a more positive way. "She got the gift I have to give," she said to Wayne. "I think she now knows there is a difference between grieving and feeling sorry for yourself. There is verbiage with pity—poor me, why me, and I can't do this, or I can't do that." Lois smiled. "I certainly don't feel a need to give up any time I have left to grieve about something I can't do anything about."

The Hospice nurse came daily, and the social worker once a week.

"It is difficult to remove my feelings from what is around me," Lois said to the Hospice social worker. "My loved ones hurt. I hear it in their voices and see it from their tears. Generally I can comfort people, but I know what they are feeling and see how difficult it is for them to let me go. I am not to blame for their grief, but this has been hard for me. Yes, they have pain, and yes, they are supposed to, for that is part of life, and there is nothing I can do about it. I may not be able to come to terms with this until I am nearer to getting my wings and feel less connected with earth and their pain and more connected with spirit."

The "Girlfriends" came often. They listened, and they reminisced with Lois about the happier times. Lois had been saving empty film boxes until she had over fifty. Wayne and the "Girlfriends" would fill these boxes with her ashes and put them in a basket for friends to take after her memorial service. Lois was told by one friend, "I will take your ashes and sprinkle them on the Gallatin High School football field so you will be part of the Green Wave forever." Another said, "I am going to take your ashes to the Hiwassee River," and Annemarie and Howard planned to take her ashes to Montana. The thought of being a part of so many wonderful places made Lois's heart sing.

Lois was very open with her son about her death. "I want you to know what to expect," she said. "You certainly have the right to do some grieving alone, but you will need to share with other people. The more you talk to others, the more the healing happens. You will eventually have to tell people your mother died, and facing those circumstances and saying how you feel is how the heart heals.

"One of the things that makes grieving harder is when people feel guilty about things they should have done or didn't do. We have had some rough times in the past. I would not want you to feel guilty because we have done a really good job catching up with each other. I hope you know that I made mistakes with you as a mother. I am sorry for those mistakes. They were not planned and not malicious, but they were made out of my ignorance, and I am deeply sorry."

"I am in a better place than I was when I was fourteen," Paul III said, and his mother smiled.

"I am so glad to hear you say that," Lois said as he gave her a hug.

"Because of this illness, I have the chance to prepare for my death, and I hope this will make it easier for you. I want you to come to this house whenever you want to be here. You will be welcome when I am sick and when I am dying. Remember there is no right way to do this. If you need to be by my bedside, I want you to be there. If you don't, that is all right too. But if you decide to stay with me and find that you must go to the bathroom and I die while you are gone, don't let that weigh heavily on your heart. Some people feel they have goofed the whole thing up if they are not there when a person dies, but if you are supposed to be there, you will be.

"There is a possibility I could go into a coma. It will be hard for you because my body will be here but my spirit won't. In that case, you should choose to be with me or not. I would probably not be having any pain or discomfort. If it does happen, I pray I will die very quickly; and under no circumstances do I want IV fluids or a feeding tube. A coma would indicate that my body was getting toxic, and there would be no sense in feeding it or prolonging the process. When I cannot communicate and life doesn't have any meaning for me in this physical body, then I am ready to leave."

Lois cried as she told him some of this, and when she finished she said, "I don't want to overwhelm you and talk about things that are so hard for you to hear that you won't want to come see me, but you know I am not taking any more chemo."

"I think you have made the right decision, and I support you." Paul III brushed tears from his eyes as he said, "I always feel better after talking with you."

Lois gave him a kiss, then asked, "How are you going to deal with it, when I die?"

"I will talk with my dad," he said. "I will get the telephone numbers of your friends."

Lois smiled, "Absolutely, and maybe, like Wayne, you will go to some of the support groups through Hospice. They know things that will be helpful," she said and reached over to touch her son.

Lois had a unique way of keeping her many friends informed of her progress. She left daily updated messages on her answering machine. "Yesterday I had abdominal pain, but this morning it is gone. This is a wonderful world. Thank you for your love and prayers."

"The meds continue to work; I am free from symptoms."—"I ran two miles today." As her illness progressed she would say, "Had some nausea this morning, but meds took care of it." Each message ended with "Thank you for your love and prayers."

The first time Wayne left the daily message, everyone who heard it panicked. Lois laughed, "I was just too involved with my work and asked him to do it." She did a few more updates, then left this task to Wayne. Her progress could be ascertained from the tone of his voice as he said, "Lois had a good night last night and is resting this morning."—"Lois is eating less, but her color is good and she is not having pain." And each messaged ended with "Thank you for your love and prayers."

He could barely speak the Friday he said, "Lois responded to my hugs this morning." And the hardest was, "The Hospice nurse said the angels were here to take Lois, and we thought it would be last night." That was Saturday morning, September 1, 2001.

And the angels did come that evening.

Lois: "Being active is no longer a part of my life, but I still have the ability to love and be loved. Love is with us forever and always. I have been given over three years of unconditional love because I have been open about my dying, and it would not have happened if I had hidden that away. My feeling is, as long as you have love, there is no reason to give up hope, especially if we recognize that birth means death. I mean that for all of us; being born means we will die.

"I have hope for the future of mankind. I won't be here, but my spirit will be, and hopefully my works will be, so the ripples each one of us makes will go on. We may never know how a piece of us has changed this world for the better. I know of times when I made a difference, but probably my greatest work came when I wasn't aware of it.

"From Radnor Lake I learned that a tree may fall, but a new one comes up somewhere and takes its place. Life goes on, and that's the way it's supposed to be. If you live while you are alive, then it doesn't matter that you die. It is so simple, just living. The waves come in and the waves go out. . . ."

AFTERWORD

Mike Rose, from NewsChannel 5, was with Lois until the very last. A beautiful, heartfelt documentary, with Amy Marsalis narrating, aired soon after Lois's death and received a terrific response. The "Living with Dying" group is still a part of Gilda's Club Nashville. The ripples Lois made continue on!

0-595-33440-7

Printed in the United States
43381LVS00004B/80